I'M SPEAKING

I'm Speaking

Every Woman's Guide to Finding Your Voice and Using It Fearlessly

Jessica Doyle-Mekkes

ROWMAN & LITTLEFIELD
Lanham • Boulder • New York • London

Published by Rowman & Littlefield
An imprint of The Rowman & Littlefield Publishing Group, Inc.
4501 Forbes Boulevard, Suite 200, Lanham, Maryland 20706
www.rowman.com

86-90 Paul Street, London EC2A 4NE

British Library Cataloguing in Publication Information Available

Library of Congress Cataloging-in-Publication Data
Names: Doyle-Mekkes, Jessica, author.
Title: I'm speaking : every woman's guide to finding your voice and using it fearlessly / Jessica Doyle-Mekkes.
Description: Lanham : Rowman & Littlefield, [2023] | Includes bibliographical references and index.
Identifiers: LCCN 2023010815 (print) | LCCN 2023010816 (ebook) | ISBN 9781538179161 (cloth) | ISBN 9781538179178 (ebook)
Subjects: LCSH: Self-confidence. | Communication.
Classification: LCC BF698.35.R47 D48 2023 (print) | LCC BF698.35.R47 (ebook) | DDC 155.2—dc23/eng/20230620
LC record available at https://lccn.loc.gov/2023010815
LC ebook record available at https://lccn.loc.gov/2023010816

For my daughters, Tallulah and Jolie:
May you always know the power of your voice and never be afraid to use it.

Contents

Introduction

This is not a book on public speaking. Public speaking is a middle-aged white guy standing in front of a podium, telling you details you don't need to know about a topic you're not all that interested in. He thinks he's funny. His mustache is funny.

This is a book about finding your voice and using it fearlessly.

Truth time: No one is going to give you what you want. You have to ask for it, and women just aren't asking. Do women want to create change? To speak up against toxic culture? To speak their truth authentically? Do women want more wealth? To grow a seven-figure business? To join the C-suite? Do women have big dreams? Life-changing, next-generation-inspiring, earth-shattering dreams? *You're damn right they do.* But somewhere between the aim and the arrival, women are getting lost.

Don't believe me? Consider this:

- Only 8 percent of women report new policies implemented at work due to the #MeToo movement.[1]
- Forty-five percent of female business leaders say it's difficult for women to speak up in meetings.[2]
- Men are four times more likely to negotiate for what they want at work.[3]
- Sixty percent of women say they've never negotiated their salary; they quit instead.[4]

- Men do 75 percent of the talking during an average business meeting.[5]

My goal is to fix this. I want to help women change their lives and the lives of those in their family, their community, their country, and the world. It's what fuels my fire and everything else I do. For me, it all starts with your voice.

The idea for this book was born because too many of the women I love—educated, professional, creative women—aren't being heard. These women know how to save lives but not how to ask for a raise. They know how to run companies but not how to handle difficult conversations. They know how to inspire children but don't believe in their own abilities. They know how to engineer complex systems but not speak confidently about their world-changing effects.

The canon of books and blogs on public speaking is huge. Clearly, if the research is telling us that Jane would rather spend her Tuesday morning shark cage diving off the Eastern Cape of South Africa, sans cage, than asking her boss of six years for the raise she *totally* deserves, there is a problem to be fixed. Many of these authors have great advice. I know; in the fifteen years I've been working with voices, I've read a lot of them. But I believe they are missing two essential pieces of the puzzle: how the brain learns and how to create change quickly. (They're also often missing content that women actually want to read; it is possible to be both educational and entertaining.)

Who am I? I'm a professor and researcher who studies the voice. I'm a vocal coach who has spent the last fifteen years working with singers, actors, and public speakers creating clear, confident, flexible, authentic voices. I'm also an actor, so I have an intimate relationship with performance anxiety.

During my first years working, my performance anxiety followed me around from audition to audition like a dark cloud—a dark cloud that a very gifted psychic above a Subway restaurant in downtown Chicago told me she could remove for $20, which, looking back, I totally should have coughed up the cash for. Instead, I dealt with my anxiety in other ways, ranging from exercise to mindfulness to once taking a Xanax before an audition to calm my nerves. The first two I highly recommend; the third not so much. Turns out it's really hard to tap dance on Xanax.

I decided I want to bridge the gap between public speaking and self-confidence for women in a new way. What you may not know about your voice is that it's made of skeletal muscle—the same kind of muscle you work in the gym—and that means that just like your peach, it can be trained. I want to teach women how to literally retrain their voices to sound clearer and more confident *while still sounding like themselves.*

I don't believe in lowering a woman's pitch so she can be heard on a microphone that was designed for a man. I don't believe that vocal fry—the gritty, gravelly sound that rose to popularity with the Kardashians and is natural for a lot of female voices—makes a woman sound annoying or unintelligent. I do believe that each woman is capable, by making small, specific changes, of speaking in a way that both reflects who she is and commands a room.

I like to say that my work is voice science, brain science, and girl power. The first four chapters of this book are voice science, the next four are brain science, and the last two are girl power. Chapters 1 through 3 address the voice, breathing, and posture for successful speaking. I'm going to clear up common misconceptions; for example, you aren't going to see me use the term "belly breathing" in this book (other than to explain why it's incorrect), because if air is entering your belly instead of your lungs, you need to put this book down and call 911 immediately.

Instead, I'm going to explain how holding the abdominal muscles in rigidly, either through your own iron will or a tight pair of Spanx, prevents your lungs from being able to fully inflate. This leaves a lot of women walking around in a constant state of hyperventilation. You might think hyperventilation occurs only during strenuous exercise or a Jason Momoa movie, but you'd be wrong.

Chapter 4 addresses common vocal concerns facing women's voices and the specific concerns you have with yours. This chapter is a buffet of exercises to adjust everything from sound quality to volume to pacing to pitch. You can take only what you need or try a bit of everything; it's totally up to you. Chapter 4 also addresses common ways women give away their power when speaking. I just really feel like you should stop apologizing; does that make sense?

The next four chapters are all about how to put your newly cultivated voice to work, starting with telling the voice in your head to shut it. We all have that voice, the "you can't do it, no one likes you, you're a failure" voice that shows up when we go after something new and sparkly. Mine is named Sheila, and she's very dramatic. When she shows up, I tell her to grab a LaCroix and take a seat in the lobby because I do not have time for that shit right now.

Once you've retrained your Sheila, it's time to retrain your brain with my Three Commandments of Conquering Fear: Prime, Pinpoint, and Power. Your brain is incredible. She's got the hottest tech in town, even better than the iPhone 14. (Sorry, Apple.) But to do her best work, a girl's gotta eat . . . and drink . . . and exercise. Brain science over the past decade has done a complete overhaul of the knowledge about how the brain learns and how you can prime your brain for learning. A primed brain makes practicing anything more effective and efficient. I know that if I'm going to dedicate any of my precious free time to something, it better be effective, it better be efficient, and it better produce results. I'm going to give you the exact tools necessary to create a clear, confident voice living within a body that isn't afraid to use it, and you won't have to practice for more than twenty minutes each day. I promise.

The final chapter of the book prepares you for real-world scenarios like speaking up against toxicity, having a difficult conversation with a friend or colleague, or giving a killer presentation. It's all the changes you've created since chapter 1 coming together and working in harmony.

If you're here because it's been a while since someone reminded you that you have a voice and that voice can move mountains—please, allow me. If you're here already feeling fierce like Michelle O. with a story to tell—please, allow me to help you speak your truth in a voice that is strong, stable, and sustainable. If you're here because you find yourself in meetings, with clients, at book club, and keep swallowing the impulse to say that you deserve a raise, you have a creative solution, and *Drinking & Tweeting* should be on the list for June, Karen—please, allow me to assure you, you absolutely do and it *absolutely* should be.

Welcome. You belong here.

—Jessica

Chapter 1

Meet Your Voice

She's Dying to Meet You

I have always believed that when you have a voice, you have an obligation to use that voice to empower others.

—Diane von Furstenberg[1]

If the eyes are the windows to the soul, the voice is its hype woman. The sound of your voice gets the audience fired up for the main event: you. Joy lives in your voice: belting your favorite tune, catching up with your girlfriends over coffee, nailing that sales pitch, or reading your kiddo's favorite bedtime story. (In my case, that's currently Danielle McLean's *Wish upon a Poopicorn*. If you also have a poop-obsessed five-year-old—or even if you don't—I highly recommend checking it out. It's everything you want it to be and more.)

Pain lives in your voice, too: having the difficult conversations, arguing with your spouse, dealing with disappointment, saying goodbye. Your voice is with you each and every moment of each and every day of your entire life, in your head and coming out of your mouth. She's your closest confidante, your biggest fan, your protector, your brand ambassador. She can be sweet or snarky, bold or tender, and, sure, sometimes she doesn't know when to shut up, but she knows you inside and out and she will always be with you.

But how much do you know about her? My guess is, not much. Women often take their voices for granted, and when they do, they are missing out on a huge opportunity to make an impact, to create change, and to get what they want! So if you've seen her around a lot but have never made a formal introduction, please, allow me.

The Voice: Where She Lives and How She Works

Take a moment and Google the image "human vocal folds." Go ahead, I'll wait. That's right, your vocal folds (or vocal cords) look an awful lot like . . . a vagina. Two strong, amazing parts of the female anatomy for one today—#winning!

In fact, your voice and your vagina are *intimately* connected.[2] The same muscular waves that power your voice in speaking and singing also power up your orgasm and the contractions of childbirth. As someone who has both spoken and sung professionally (on purpose) and given birth au naturel (*not* on purpose) I can assure you that while the waves may look the same, they do not, in fact, feel the same. So you can take that excuse for not speaking up off your list.

The voice and the vagina are so closely linked that, according to somatic sex educator and doula Stacey Ramsower, "to be disconnected from one is to shut down the other."[3] Yes, you read that correctly, no voice = no orgasm. Do I have your attention now? The physical link between the voice and the vagina is the vagus nerve, the largest nerve in the body, which wanders through the body (vagus literally means "wanderer") from the pelvic region to the brain. She's large and in charge of a lot of really important physical and emotional responses.

Your vocal folds are housed in your voice box, or larynx. To find your larynx, tilt your head back and run your fingers gently down the front of your throat until you feel the bump about halfway between your chin and your collarbone. In men, it's the Adam's apple, and, while women can have an Adam's apple, too, it's usually not as pronounced and should definitely be called something else. I like "Eve's apple" because the female voice causes all sorts of trouble, especially for old white men and their gated communities.

The primary role of the larynx is airway protection.[4] At the top of the larynx is a leaf-shaped flap of cartilage, the epiglottis, which is the guard dog of your airway. When you swallow, the epiglottis lowers to cover your trachea or windpipe, sending whatever you're swallowing down the esophagus to your stomach.

Should the epiglottis fail, your vocal folds can close tightly together, blocking the entrance to your airway, and then release built-up air pressure to "forcefully expectorate," or cough up, the lodged object. Your vocal folds also perform the Valsalva maneuver, which may sound like a series of intricate acrobatic movements made famous by a pint-sized Russian gymnast but is actually a breathing technique that increases pressure in the chest, often used to unclog your ears, lift heavy things, and poop.[5]

The larynx's other job—*almost* but not quite equally important to keeping you alive—is communication. The ability to express our thoughts and emotions through language is what separates us from the animals (well, that and our ability to accessorize). When you speak or sing, air pressure builds up below your vocal folds, and when that pressure is released, the folds vibrate like a guitar string. These vibrations create sound waves, which make their way up your throat and out of your mouth.

If you didn't have a head, the air sent through your vocal folds would sound like a duck call or the mouthpiece of a trumpet (without the trumpet). Luckily, you have a head, and the spaces and structures within your head—your sinuses, teeth, tongue, jaw, and velum (the squishy part at the back of your throat that goes up when you yawn)—all work to shape that duck call into the words you speak.

The larynx is mostly made up of cartilage and skeletal muscle, the same kind of muscle you work in the gym. This means you can train your voice to increase its strength, stamina, and flexibility. It also means that to remain in tip-top shape and avoid injury, your voice needs to be warmed up before being put to work and cooled down afterward.

Now, you might be thinking, "Injury? How am I going to injure my voice? I'm not filling coliseums three hundred days a year, belting my face off for thousands of screaming thirty-something moms drunk on cheap rosé and childless freedom. I'm not Britney, bitch." In fact, one out of every thirteen adults in the United States experiences a voice disorder annually.[6]

A voice disorder occurs when your voice can't meet your daily needs.[7] Now, this might not be a big deal if you're, say, a mime on the streets of "Gay Paree," but it's a really big deal when you have to pitch a multimillion-dollar business idea, meet with a new client to discuss her dream wedding, or be able to yell, mom-style, when your five-year-old goes rogue at the park and heads into oncoming traffic. (Don't even get me started if your job includes the phrase "cleared for takeoff" or "scalpel.")

If you regularly corral a pack of feral ten-year-olds, you're at higher risk. Teachers are estimated to be two to three times more likely than the general population to develop a voice disorder,[8] which makes sense when you consider that one of the leading causes of a voice disorder is overuse of the voice: yelling, screaming, and talking too high or low in pitch.[9]

I don't only want to keep your voice injury free, I also want to keep it in tip-top shape, like JLo and Shakira, Superbowl LVI, skin-tight-metallics-on-moms-over-forty kind of shape. That voice is clear, flexible, and sustainable. That voice is also one you are in control of and can depend upon.

So, in the words of '90s country music queen Shania Twain, "Let's go, girls."

Vocal Warmups

Remember the last time you went for a run or hit the gym without warming up and stretching? Me too. It was yesterday. My alarm rang at 5:00 a.m. and I sprang out of bed, pulled on my color-coordinated workout clothes, and hit the pavement at a pace that would make Flo-Jo proud. Kidding. I did go for a morning run without warming up, but it was after hitting snooze three times, wearing sweats and a T-shirt scavenged from the bathroom floor, and at a pace that ranked somewhere between osteoporosis-afflicted octogenarian and garden slug.

It took me forever to get my mind and body going, and my legs felt like lead. Part of this is because I'm a queso-addicted mother of a one-year-old who stays up way too late watching reality shows, but the other part is because I didn't take the time to warm up. According to the Mayo Clinic (who I tend to believe), "Warming up helps prepare your body for aerobic activity. A warmup gradually revs up your cardiovascular system by raising your body temperature and increasing blood flow to your muscles. Warming up may also help reduce muscle soreness and lessen your risk of injury."[10]

Since the muscles that make up your voice are the same kind of muscles you work in the gym, your voice benefits from a warm-up just as much as your hamstrings do. The goal is to gently get your voice going and prepare it for the day ahead. Warming up your voice is simple and doesn't take a lot of time. In fact, it can be done in the shower or in the car on your way to work. (Bonus embarrassing-mom points if you drop your kids off at school while doing vocal warmups.)

Semi-Occluded Vocal Tract Exercises

Semi-occluded vocal tract exercises (SOVTEs) are an excellent way to effectively and efficiently warm up your voice. Semi-occluded is a fancy way of saying "making sound with your mouth partially closed."

Each year I invite the master's students in the speech language pathology program to give a workshop on vocal health to my musical theatre freshmen. In addition to putting the fear of the vocal-health gods into them with videos of vocal nodules and polyps, the master's students introduce SOVTEs. Their professor, who graciously accompanies them, always gives my all-time favorite description of how SOVTEs work: "If you think of speaking or singing as sitting on a swing and pumping your legs to get going, SOVTEs are like someone giving you a push."

SOVTEs make your voice more efficient and less prone to fatigue.[11] They're also great for those mornings you wake up sounding like a whiskey troll.

Straw Hums

Straw hums are the perfect way to wake up your voice and keep it feeling and sounding great throughout the day. On your next Starbucks run, grab an extra straw. Put the straw in your mouth and hum like you normally would. Then try:

1. Sirens: Slide from the lowest part of your range to the highest and back again, like a fire truck siren.
2. Hills: These are smaller sirens that gradually get larger. Imagine dividing your siren into quarters. Your first hill is just up and down one quarter. Your second goes halfway up and down. Your third is three-quarters. For the fourth hill, hum through your full siren.
3. Hum Along: Pick your favorite song and straw hum it. Bonus points if it's a power ballad. Celine Dion through a straw? Yes, please.

Helpful Hints:

1. Try not to let any air escape. You want all the air going through the straw.

2. Focus on the vibrations, not the sound. Humming through a straw is never going to be as loud as your normal voice.
3. No straw? No problem. You can hum, bubble your lips motorboat style, or buzz a "V" or "Z" sound instead.

Aim for about fifteen minutes of straw hums throughout the day, or two to three minutes, five times per day. I recommend doing them when you wake up; on the way to work; before any important meeting, presentation, or conversation; and before you go to bed. Straw work is the little black dress of vocal exercises: It's quick and easy, you can do it anywhere, and it leaves you sounding fabulous.

Blowing Bubbles

Another SOVTE you can try is blowing bubbles through a straw into a glass of water. The concept is the same as straw hums—warming up the voice without added strain—but the water gives you a visual indication of whether or not you're keeping the hum, and your breath, consistent. Fill a glass or paper cup halfway with water, grab your straw, then try:

1. Just Air: Practice starting and stopping the bubbles without humming. The goal is to keep the bubbles forming at a consistent rate throughout each exhale.
2. Humming Bubbles: Try adding a hum to your bubbles. You can do hills, sirens, or a song melody. See if you can keep the bubbles forming consistently while humming.

Helpful Hints:

1. If you're having trouble humming and blowing bubbles at the same time, try holding your nose with your free hand and be sure your lips are firmly pursed around the straw so no air can escape.

2. Try humming through the straw first, then put it in the water and add bubbles.

3. Try humming without the straw. Hum with closed lips, then open your mouth slightly as if you were going to wrap your lips around a straw. Use your free hand to feel the air coming out of your mouth. Now put the straw in your mouth and into the water, pushing the air and the hum in the same way.

Tongue Stretches

When you get up in the morning, along with stretching your neck and shoulders, try stretching your tongue. Your tongue is the primary muscle for articulation, and keeping it flexible and free ensures that your words, particularly the consonant sounds in them, are crisp and easily understood. To give your tongue a good stretch, try:

1. In and Out: Open your mouth and stick your tongue out as far as it will go. Inhale, then exhale. Now place the tip of your tongue as far back into your mouth as it will go. You should be able to touch the back of your throat, also known as the oropharynx. Inhale, then exhale. Repeat three to five times.

2. Large Circles: Open your mouth wide and use your tongue to trace three large clockwise circles around your lips. Wipe your spit, then repeat three times counterclockwise.

3. Small Circles: Open your mouth slightly and circle your tongue three times clockwise as if you are writing the letter *O*. Repeat three times counterclockwise.

4. Tongue Arch: Open your mouth wide. Anchor the tip of your tongue to your bottom teeth. Now push out with the back of your tongue so it arches up. Hold for three to five breaths.

Hydration

I'm sure you know the importance of staying hydrated, and telling you to drink water throughout the day is not new information. What you may not know is how vital hydration is to your voice.

Your vocal folds are made up of layers. There's some muscle at the bottom and some epithelial (skin-like) cells on the top covered by a shmear of mucus, and in between is a Jell-O-like substance called the lamina propria.[12] It's the jiggle of this Jell-O that creates a clear, brilliant, healthy sound when you speak, and for your Jell-O to jiggle, it needs water.

Hold your hands out in front of you, about six inches apart, palms facing each other. Begin to gently clap your hands together. That's speaking. Clap them harder. That's speaking loudly. Clap them really hard. That's yelling. Now, imagine doing this one hundred times per second, like your vocal folds do. Even gentle clapping will eventually cause your hands to start stinging. So how do your vocal folds do it? Well, other than being one of the superheroes of the human body, they rely on a thin layer of mucus that keeps them flexible and lubricated so they can vibrate safely.[13]

The vocal folds don't have their own hydration and lubrication system, so keeping the Jell-O jiggly and the mucus thin and watery is completely dependent on you keeping your body hydrated.[14]

Unfortunately, drinking a glass of water five minutes before your presentation isn't going to cut it. It takes about four hours for the water you drink to hydrate your vocal folds.[15] So rather than hydrating specifically for a meeting or interview, it's best to simply stay hydrated. Pee pale. Whizz white. You know the drill. Where this gets tricky is if you have to be ready to speak early in the morning. You lose around two pounds of water weight each night simply through breathing, so when you wake up in the morning, your body is pretty dehydrated.[16] So is your voice. A dehydrated voice may sound raspy, breathy, and dull. Dehydration also reduces mucus production, increasing the chance for swelling, irritation, and injury.[17]

The solution? When you wake up, immediately drink a glass of water. Want to level up? Set an alarm for 5:00 a.m., wake up, drink a glass of water, and then go back to bed. Hydration achievement unlocked.

It has long been thought that coffee is dehydrating because caffeine is a diuretic. (That means it makes you pee.) However, in what I consider to be one of—if not *the*—most important scientific breakthroughs in recent years (along with Duke University's successful in-captivity hibernation of the fat-tailed dwarf lemur, obviously), voice science research has now proven otherwise! A study out of the School of Sport and Exercise Sciences at the University of Birmingham compared the dehydrating effects of moderate coffee drinking (three to six cups per day) versus water and found *no evidence* that drinking coffee makes you pee any more than drinking plain water does.[18] Power to the planet's favorite wet bean.

Get Steamy

Walk into your local pharmacy, and you'll see a variety of products designed to coat your throat and soothe your voice. Teas, lozenges, and sprays may make your sore throat feel better, but they do absolutely nothing—I repeat, *absolutely nothing*—to help your voice. Why? Because when you swallow, your epiglottis covers the entrance to your larynx, sending your tea/lozenge/spray down your esophagus and into your digestive tract.[19] Your magic potion of choice never touches your vocal folds. If it did, you'd be choking.

So what do you do if you're feeling tired, hoarse, or under the weather but you still have to use your voice? It's time to get steamy. Steam is inhaled, so it makes direct contact with your vocal folds.[20] Close your eyes and transport yourself to the steam room at a fancy day spa. Feel the mist as it floats down and lands on your body. It's warm. It's gentle. It soothes your tired muscles and relaxes you from head to toe. Then you hear the door open, and in walks Jason Momoa wearing nothing but Kal Drogo eyeliner and a smile. I'm going to let you pause and enjoy this moment. Continue whenever you're ready. Take your time.

All that steamy goodness relaxes and soothes your vocal folds too. Not only does it feel great, inhaling steam has also been scientifically proven to improve vocal health and hygiene.[21]

You can purchase a sinus/facial steamer for about fifty bucks. I own the Vicks Sinus Inhaler and use it without the menthol inserts. It works with just tap water and takes about six minutes to heat up. I'll steam for fifteen to twenty minutes in the mornings when I'm feeling like my voice could use a little extra love or on days when I have a big speaking event. You can also take a long, steamy shower or go totally old school and boil a pot of water, throw a towel over your head, put your head above the pot, and breathe.

Your Vocal Health Routine

Have you ever been in really great shape, then gone on vacation and returned to the gym to find you're winded during workouts that used to be easy? If you have, you've experienced the exercise principle of reversibility or detrainability—the "if you don't use it, you lose it" principle—and it applies to your voice too.[22] As you start using the tools in this chapter and throughout this book, you will hear and feel positive changes in your voice. Making those changes permanent is up to you. It takes about sixty-six days to form a routine; physical routines, like exercise, can take longer.[23]

So get in the habit of taking care of your voice now. Have a glass of water when you wake up. Keep a straw in your car to warm up your voice on the way to work. Linger in a hot shower a little longer, and when your teenager asks for the third time if you're out of the bathroom yet, explain that it's for your vocal health. You're welcome to blame me; I can take it.

It's also important to be aware of the behaviors that can harm your voice. Your voice doesn't have a carrying case. If it did, mine would definitely be a crocodile Birkin bag in a very loud shade of magenta, which I would be impulsively drawn to and then later regret purchasing because it goes with absolutely nothing in my wardrobe. (Yes, I have given this some thought.) But it doesn't have a carrying case. So you have to take care of her.

We've already talked about what to do, so here's what not to do.

Misuse/Overuse

Remember the last time you got rowdy at a concert or sporting event? Did you wake up the next morning to a hoarse, croaky voice? If the answer is yes, then you were suffering from what we in the voice biz call a phonotrauma.

Phonotraumas happen when we push our voices beyond what they're comfortably or typically used to.[24] Remember earlier in the chapter when I had you clap your hands together to mimic the collision of your vocal folds? Hard, continuous clapping makes your hands sting, turn red, and, over time, start to swell. An evening of screaming at your ten-year-old to "get back on defense" does the same thing to your vocal folds. The swelling from one night of overuse isn't usually too big a deal; you might sound hoarse the next day, and you'll need to rest your voice so that it can recover. But repeated events of overuse? Molly, you in danger, girl.

Think of your heels rubbing against the backs of the four-inch, peep-toe, glossy black patent leather pumps that you *had* to have even though they were just a little too big. First your heels turn red. Wear the shoes all day and you're looking at a blister situation. Keep wearing them and that blister is going to become a callus. It's the same thing with your vocal folds. Repeated events of overuse can result in blisters (called polyps) and calluses (called nodules).[25]

Vocal fold polyps and nodules can cause your voice to constantly sound hoarse, breathy, or rough.[26] They can also be painful. Once they occur, you're probably going to need voice therapy, and in extreme cases, they may have to be surgically removed.[27]

You might be thinking, "I go to a concert maybe once a year, and I can bring a cowbell and several thoughtfully worded signs to next Friday's game, which will embarrass my kid more than my yelling at her. This is totally a win-win." And you're right, absolutely. But it's also important to be mindful of the day-to-day situations that can cause phonotrauma.

A few years ago, I had a client who started a new job working the front desk at a gym. She'd come in for her sessions with me and be frustrated because her voice wasn't sounding as clear and strong as she knew it could. I asked her about any changes in her life, and she mentioned her new position. Turns out, the gym's loud music combined with her job of greeting guests and checking them in was causing her to speak louder than her voice was comfortable with. In the moment, she didn't notice that she was talking too loudly, but by the end of her shift she was hoarse.

Work in a loud restaurant or bar? Teach young kids? Spend hours in virtual meetings? There's a good chance you're overusing your voice without realizing it. The National Institute on Deafness and Other Communication Disorders reports an estimated 17.9 million adults in the United States report problems with their voice each year,[28] and women have been found to experience vocal health problems more frequently than men, regardless of occupation.[29]

Why? Well, first, there's hormones. Studies suggest the female voice is affected by hormone fluctuations during menstruation and menopause.[30] As a woman who uses her voice professionally and has gotten her period every month for the last twenty-seven years (minus my pregnancies), I can attest that this statement is accurate. Science says this is because the mucus changes in the vocal folds mimic those in the vagina,[31] which is extremely gross.

I say it's because one week a month my entire body swells to such manatee-like proportions that an entire portion of my closet has been dedicated to tentlike cotton dresses in an array of blacks that may or may not have been purchased from the sleepwear department at Target. I feel like shit. I look like shit. It's not shocking that I don't sound my best either.

If you're a living, breathing woman between the ages of birth and death, I'm willing to bet you have experienced anxiety at some point in your life; in fact, science tells us that beginning with puberty and extending through their childbearing years, women deal with anxiety and depression more than men do.[32] If this is shocking to you, refer to the previous paragraph, then binge-watch *PEN15*, *Girls*, and *Working Moms*, in that order, immediately.

Prolonged anxiety and emotional stress are major contributing factors in muscle tension dysphonia, a voice disorder where the muscles of the larynx tense or tighten more than they should.[33] Muscle tension dysphonia causes the voice to consistently sound hoarse, breathy, or gravelly.[34] It can also cause the voice to "give out" or become weaker as it's used throughout the day.

Once muscle tension dysphonia develops, it doesn't just go away, even once the initial trigger is gone.[35] Fixing it often requires voice therapy, overseen by a speech language pathologist, to alleviate throat tension and restore the voice to health.

Before I tell you the final reason—which is not *the* final reason but the last one I'm going to cover—I need to point out that before writing this chapter, I wasn't aware of this particular scientific gem. I was aware of increased anxiety among women, and, as I have gotten in my car on the first day of my period knowing there's a fifty-fifty chance I will end up with either french fries or a felony charge, I was aware of the hormonal roller coaster that is womanhood, but this I was unaware of. And she's a doozy. Drumroll, please.

A study out of Salt Lake City proposed that women experience more vocal health problems than men because our bodies contain more fat and, therefore, less water than a man's, which may leave us more susceptible to systemic dehydration.[36] Are you kidding me? I am not. Women's bodies are 50 percent water, compared to men's 59 percent, and that difference of 9 percent is due to body fat (or, in my case, due to cheese). You already know that a dehydrated body equals a dehydrated voice. Sure, starting your sales pitch sounding like a bourbon ogre is going to capture your audience's attention, but I'm pretty sure you want them thinking your idea is worthy of a seven-figure investment, not wondering what's wrong with you and if it's contagious.

Before you start thinking, "So, I'm an anxious, hormonal mess with a slight double chin and chafing thighs who's now also on the brink of vocal demise? Wow. Thank you for pointing that out. I'm so glad I picked up this book"—listen up. Women do not succeed because we do not face tough shit. We succeed in spite of it.

You know who has been diagnosed with endometriosis and PCOS? Jillian Michaels.[37] Yes, Jillian "You're not going to die; you've been through worse" Michaels, the world's foremost fitness expert, best-selling author, and all-around badass Mama Jama. You know who has a speech impediment? Amanda Gorman.[38] The youngest inaugural poet in US history has both an auditory processing disorder and a speech impediment and credits them as one of her greatest strengths. You know who suffers from depression? Oprah.[39] Enough said. Now imagine a world where these women chose to stay silent because the biological deck was stacked against them. Yeah, I don't want to, either.

The thing is you don't need to look to the Oprahs of the world to find these voices. Do you know a mother whose voice isn't essential? Let's expand that. Do you know a *woman* whose voice isn't essential to her career, her family, her community, the world? Imagine a world without the voices of your mother, your best girlfriend, your midwife, your hair stylist. I don't know about you, but I'd be an uninspired puddle of loneliness with postpartum PTSD and a really unfortunate asymmetrical bob.

Summary

- If the eyes are the window to the soul, the voice is its hype woman. The sound of your voice matters just as much, if not more, than the words you're saying. Sounding hoarse, groggy, or like your preferred breakfast consists of six Pall Malls and a Bloody Mary may have your audience worrying less about the problem at hand and more about what's wrong with you and if they can catch it.
- Your voice box, or larynx, houses your vocal folds. Like strings on a guitar, your vocal folds vibrate to create sound, and that sound then travels up into your head where it's shaped into words.
- The same muscle contractions that power up your vocal folds also power up your orgasm, and according to somatic sex educator and doula Stacey Ramsower, "to be disconnected from one is to shut down the other." No voice = no orgasm (as if you needed a reminder).
- The muscles that make up your voice are the same kind of muscles you work in the gym, so your voice benefits from a warmup just as much as your hamstrings do. The goal is to gently get your voice going and prepare it for the day ahead.
- SOVTEs such as humming, lip buzzes, straw hums, and blowing bubbles are excellent ways to warm up your voice. Aim for two to three minutes, five times per day.
- Hydrate. Your voice doesn't have its own hydration system, so maintaining your body's hydration is important. It takes about four hours for the water you drink to hydrate your vocal folds, so drink early and often.
- Get steamy. Teas, lozenges, and sprays may make your throat feel better, but they don't do anything for your vocal folds because, thanks to the epiglottis, they never touch

them. Steam does, and it's a fantastic way to soothe your voice when it's tired or you're under the weather. Invest in a personal steamer or just take a long, hot shower with the bathroom door closed.

- Misuse/overuse is a common reason for vocal fold injuries. If you work in a loud environment or spend a lot of time on Zoom, try wearing a single earplug while working. You'll have a much better idea of how loud you're speaking, which is probably louder than you need to.
- Hormones, anxiety, body composition . . . thanks to biology, women are at higher risk for voice injuries than men are, regardless of occupation. Many women don't think about their voices until they need them and they aren't there, so put a vocal health routine in place now to keep your voice in tip-top shape.

Chapter 2

Just Breathe

During my first vocal jury (a final exam where the student performs the pieces they've been working on that semester) in grad school, a professor told me, "The breath is supposed to relax the body and energize the voice." Actually, his complete statement was, "The breath is supposed to relax the body and energize the voice. Yours does neither." Not my proudest moment, though it definitely paled in comparison to forgetting the words to a song I'd been working on for the past three months, four times, in the same spot. It's really hard to ad lib in Italian.

I'm very proud to say that in the years since, I've become a much better breather, but I've held on to his words and often use them when working with clients. I've also held on to the other lesson I learned that day: Fear is a nasty bitch. Taking the stage to sing that day, I was scared.

See, I went back to grad school at the age of thirty-one, which made me at least seven years older than most of the other graduate students, who were still drinking wine with words like "Hawaiian" on the label and living the good life on their parents' health insurance. My decision to go back to school was fueled by my desire to teach in higher ed, and even though I had nearly a decade of experience and had worked with some *really* big-name singers, the required box next to "master's degree" remained unchecked.

When I decided to pursue this goal, it was under two conditions: (1) I could commute and simultaneously run my voice studio, which was flourishing, and (2) I got it paid for. With my conditions met, I started a master's program in classical singing, which I prepared for by spending three months working with a classical voice coach but otherwise knew absolutely nothing about. During my first lesson, my voice professor, who remains a dear friend and mentor, asked me, "So what songs have you worked on?"—to which I answered, "The four I auditioned with."

The hardest thing about going back to school as an adult, other than realizing I knew how to neither Whip nor Nae Nae, is that I was already an established professional. I knew how to sing. I knew how to coach singers. I knew I was good at both things. I had been paid—a lot—to do both things. So going back to square one and having to relearn how to do what I had been successfully doing for years, but in a very different way, was humbling. To then present my new (and very unsteady) skills after my first semester to a room of classical music professors with clipboards and red pens at the ready was terrifying.

What I didn't realize at the time was that forgetting my words, four times, in exactly the same place, was the result of my body's response to fear. And a big part of that was my breathing—or lack thereof.

Every Breath You Take

Your breath is one of your most important tools for success when speaking. Every breath you take (yes, I sing this, à la Sting, whenever I work with a client on breathing) is not only a chance to relax your body and energize your voice; it's also a chance to regain control. Need to get your train of thought back on the tracks? Take a breath. Want to emphasize an important point or wait for a response? Take a breath. Need to calm your racing heart and still your shaking legs? That's right—breathe.

Inadequate breath support, or not having enough air, can show up as heavy breathing or gasping for air while speaking; tension in the chest, neck, and shoulders; a lack of volume, particularly at the ends of phrases; and a lack of energy in the voice.[1] It also increases anxiety.

In his book *Breath: The New Science of a Lost Art*, author James Nestor talks about the relationship between breathing and anxiety: "Breathing, as it happens, is more than just a biochemical or physical act; it's more than just moving the diaphragm downward and sucking in air to feed hungry cells and remove wastes. . . . Breathing is a power switch to a vast network called the autonomic nervous system."[2]

The autonomic nervous system has three parts: the sympathetic nervous system, the parasympathetic nervous system, and the enteric nervous system. The sympathetic nervous system is the gas pedal for your body's fight-or-flight response, while the parasympathetic nervous system, known as the rest-and-digest system, is the brake.[3]

The sympathetic nervous system enlarges your pupils to let more light in, increases your heart rate, and slows digestion so energy can be used in other parts of the body.[4] Basically, it's Madeline Kahn as Gussie Mausheimer in *An American Tail*, yelling, "Release the secret weapon!" as the mice of New York prepare for battle against the city's cats. (That reference is for my mom. Love you, Jules.)

The blissed-out feeling you get after a spa day of being soaked, wrapped, and kneaded like a side of Gold Ring Wagyu? Thank your parasympathetic nervous system. This little baby also makes your mouth water before a delicious meal, has you tearing up at your little sister's wedding, and revs your engine before sex.

Your lungs are covered with nerves that connect to the autonomic nervous system, and most of the connections to the parasympathetic system are on the lower parts of the lobes.[5] Deep breathing activates the parasympathetic nervous system; it helps you calm down. The slower and deeper you breathe, the more powerful the parasympathetic nervous system's response is and the calmer you become. Yes, when Daniel Tiger sings, "Take a deep breath and count to four," he's actually giving sound advice in parasympathetic nervous system activation, which is pretty impressive for a tiger who is constantly experiencing first world preschool problems and never wears pants.

Conversely, the majority of the nerves connecting to the sympathetic nervous system are spread out at the top of the lungs.[6] Taking short, rapid breaths is a distress call; you're basically sending up a smoke signal to your brain saying, "Rally the troops; winter is coming and it's bringing a dragon." The longer this rapid, short breathing goes on, the stronger the call gets. This is super helpful if you are, indeed, in imminent danger, but not so helpful when you're giving a presentation or in the middle of an important conversation.

It takes only a split second for the sympathetic nervous system to kick into high gear, but it takes an hour or more for the parasympathetic nervous system to return the body to neutral.[7] This is why it's important to get the parasympathetic nervous system going before you need it. Breathing slowly and deeply, filling your lungs all the way to the bottom, before and during your speaking event, signals to your brain that all is well. There's no need for panic. You are a pool of tranquility.

Basic Breathing Test

The sympathetic nervous system is meant to be activated in short bursts, when danger is present, not to be continuously running the show. When there's an imbalance between fight-or-flight and rest-and-digest it can lead to a host of really unpleasant things, including blood pressure complications, cardiac distress, and problems breathing and swallowing.[8]

Living in a state of stress may mean you are also living in a state of hyperventilation. Hyperventilation is best known as the acute response to panic attacks, extreme exercise, and the Magic Mike series, but there's another type of hyperventilation—chronic hyperventilation—that is far more common and far less noticeable.[9] Below is my Basic Breathing Test, based on the Nijmegen questionnaire, a screening tool used to detect dysfunctional breathing patterns.[10] Number a piece of paper 1–16, then rate each corresponding term accordingly: Never: 0, Rarely: 1, Sometimes: 2, Often: 3. Total your answers and see below for your results.

How often do you feel:

1. Chest Pain
2. Feeling Tense
3. Blurred Vision
4. Dizzy Spells
5. Feeling Confused
6. Faster/Deeper Breathing
7. Short of Breath
8. Tight Feeling in Chest
9. Bloated Feeling in Stomach
10. Tingling Fingers
11. Unable to Breathe Deeply
12. Stiff Fingers or Arms
13. Tight Feelings around Mouth
14. Cold Hands or Feet
15. Palpitations
16. Feelings of Anxiety

Results:

- 23 or higher: Molly, you in danger, girl. It is likely that you have a dysfunctional breathing pattern that is negatively affecting your mental, physical, emotional, and vocal health.
- 19–23: Some bad habits. It is likely that you have developed some dysfunctional breathing habits and would benefit from retraining how you breathe.
- 15–19: Time to breathe up to your potential. While not dysfunctional, your breathing habits could be better.
- 10–14: She's a B student. Your breathing is pretty good. Still, you may want to look into breath training for maintenance and further improvement.
- 0–10: Congratulations! You are a champion breather!

Scared by your score? The rest of this chapter is full of exercises to help you create some new, healthier breathing habits. Already a breathing queen? Stick around and show off a little.

Breath Work

When I was in the eighth grade, my best friend taught me her secret to looking skinny. She stood in front of her bathroom mirror and gripped the countertop with both hands. "Breathe in," she said, sucking her belly in as far as was humanly possible; "Breathe out," she said, releasing it. Then she said, "Breathe in . . . okay, now don't breathe out." Or at least I think that's what she said. It was hard to tell because she had sucked her belly in so hard, I was afraid her intestines were now somewhere near her throat. She did look thinner. And redder. And she couldn't walk very fast because there was barely any oxygen getting to her body. But thinner, check!

Here's a hot tip for the following exercises (and life): Sucking it in really sucks. Your belly is meant to go out when you breathe.

Assess Your Breath

Sit tall and place one hand on your belly and the other on your chest.

- Take a few normal breaths and notice how your hands are moving.
- When you inhale, which hand moves more? Chest or belly?
- Are you breathing through your nose or your mouth?
- Is your torso expanding (like a balloon inflating) when you inhale and contracting when you exhale?

Red Flags

- The chest hand moves more than the belly hand.
- The chest hand moves before the belly hand.
- The belly hand moves in on inhalation (contracting) rather than out (expanding).

Quick Fix

If you noticed more movement in your chest or a contracting motion on the inhale, try this: Lean forward in your chair, resting your elbows on your knees and your chin on the backs of your hands. Take a few deep breaths and focus on feeling your belly expand on the inhale and contract on the exhale. Once that movement feels comfortable, try sitting up, then standing.

Hold Up . . . Breathe

Remember holding your breath as a kid? Turns out, being comfortable holding your breath, or withholding breath, is important as an adult too. When your brain senses a lack of air, it goes into panic mode, causing you to hyperventilate, and there is nothing like gasping for air mid-presentation to make a girl feel like she's totally in control. Am I right? To stay cool as a cucumber, you need to get comfortable with being hungry for air.

Hot Tip: You. Will. Not. Die. It is *impossible* to empty all the air out of your lungs. But it is *very* possible to go into panic mode because you feel like you can't catch your breath.

Here we go . . .

- Sit down and relax for a few minutes before starting this exercise.
- Breathe normally. Once you exhale, hold your nose.
- Time yourself. How long can you hold your breath comfortably?
- When you feel the strong desire to breathe, release your nose.
- Did you gulp air when you started breathing again? Then you went a bit too long. Try to make the first breath you take a normal through-the-nose, belly-out inhalation.

Results:

- 40+ seconds: Congratulations! You are a champion breather!
- 30–40 seconds: Pretty damn good. Way to go.
- 20–30 seconds: She's borderline.
- Less than 20: Threat detected. Your brain definitely sees even a small increase in CO_2 as an immediate threat. Cue panic mode.

Scared of your score? The next exercise is geared toward retraining your brain to panic less when CO_2 levels rise. Give it a try, then see if your score here improves.

Rectangle Breathing

Have you heard of box breathing? Rectangle breathing is like that, with shorter inhales and longer exhales. Thus, the rectangle.

This exercise will meet you where you're at, so sit, stand, lay on the floor, walk your dog, whatever.

- Inhale for a three count through your nose. Don't suck in air like someone's going to take it away from you, just a normal inhale.
- Exhale through your mouth on a "shhhh" sound (think a leaky tire) for a nine count.
- Repeat: in for three, out for nine, for ten rounds.
- Try to keep the inhales normal.

Repeat "Hold Up . . . Breathe" and see if your numbers improve. You may find that after this exercise, slightly rising CO_2 levels don't cause your brain to enter panic mode as quickly—or at all.

If this exercise works for you, use it! It's the perfect prep for a presentation, meeting, interview, holiday with your in-laws . . . any stressful situation. If you're in public and don't want to sound like a leaky tire, you can also exhale through your nose. Sneaky, sneaky.

Belly Breathing

When talking about breathing and breath work, the term "diaphragmatic breathing," or "belly breathing," gets thrown around a lot. I want to break this term down, because it's one many of my clients don't truly understand, but they don't want to look stupid or like they don't pay attention in yoga class, so they pretend to.

Place your hands, palm sides down, on your chest between your collarbone and your nipples. If your hands don't fit there because your boobs are just that perky, screw you (and I'd like the name of your plastic surgeon). Under your hands, inside your rib cage, are your lungs. You breathe into and out of your lungs. Not your diaphragm. Not your belly. Not your toes. Not your honey pot.

Your diaphragm is a dome-shaped muscle that separates your chest from your abdomen. It's large and very thin, about the width of a piece of card stock. (Fun fact: If you've had skirt steak, you've eaten a cow's diaphragm.) At rest, your diaphragm lives up under your lower ribs, where it's protected in case you take a spear to the chest. When you inhale, the diaphragm contracts and creates the vacuum that pulls air into your lungs. If your abs are not rigidly held in, the diaphragm will fully contract down into your abdomen, pushing your guts out of the way and causing your belly to go out. Thus, "belly breathing."

Yes, diaphragmatic breathing and belly breathing are just super-sexy terms for the natural way you breathe. Trouble brews when the abs are held in too tightly, preventing the diaphragm from fully contracting and the lungs from fully filling with air. Then, instead of the natural in-and-out motion of the belly, the chest and shoulders start to go up and down.

Not only does this mean the lungs aren't fully expanding and the nerve endings of the parasympathetic nerve system aren't being activated, but it causes unnecessary tension in the upper body. Tension is the murderer of vibration, and making sound, like talking, is all about vibration. Unnecessary tension in the shoulders and jaw (clench your teeth much?) is like putting wet clay on a guitar string. Just like a rock star will have to work harder to get the stairway all the way to heaven, you'll have to work harder to be heard, especially if you're trying to fill a large room without amplification.

Other Places of Expansion

You already know that when you take a full, deep breath, your diaphragm contracts, pushing your guts and belly out, and your lungs inflate, causing your rib cage and chest to expand. The chest and belly are the two most common places to feel movement when breathing, but there is also a third place: the pelvic floor.

If you're unfamiliar with the muscles of your pelvic floor, you clearly have never had to cross your legs while laughing to keep from wetting yourself. (Side note: My mom used to do this all the time when I was a kid, and I thought it was hilarious. One of my favorite games was trying to get her to laugh so hard she would pee her pants, particularly when in public. Now that I've given birth to two babies, I see how ridiculously cruel this was. My deepest apologies.)

For real, though, if you are unfamiliar with these muscles, go ahead and pretend you are trying to hold in a really big fart. Don't clench with your buns or tummy muscles; focus on the muscles down under. Welcome to your pelvic floor.

Think of your abdominal cavity from the diaphragm at the top to the pelvic floor at the bottom as a big piston: When there are movement and pressure changes at the top, there must be movement and pressure changes at the bottom.[11] When you inhale and the diaphragm contracts, the muscles of the pelvic floor stretch. When you exhale and the diaphragm releases up into the rib cage, the muscles of the pelvic floor rise.

Your pelvic floor muscles are working at low levels pretty much all day long, providing support for the organs in your pelvis and keeping you from peeing your pants. When you inhale deeply, the stretch in the pelvic floor muscles gives them a nice little break. If your diaphragm isn't contracting fully on your inhale, either because your breath is too shallow or your abdominal muscles are held in too tightly, the pelvic floor muscles don't get to stretch. Overly tense pelvic floor muscles may lead to pelvic pain, urinary incontinence, and overactive bladder syndrome.[12]

Basically, if the muscles don't get their break, they get pissed. Can you blame them? I've been writing this chapter for two hours and I've already taken breaks to stretch, get another cup of coffee, and check @dogsofinstagram, twice.

Now, you might be thinking, "Wow, three places of expansion; that's a lot to think about. What if my belly really moves but my rib cage doesn't? What if I don't feel any action in my pelvic floor? What if my rib cage is expanding but my six-pack is super toned and staying put?" Fear not. Every body is different, so every body is going to expand a little differently. Where you feel the most expansion isn't nearly as important as whether or not you are expanding. As long as your shoulders aren't going up and down and you're not gripping the bathroom counter in an effort to pull your intestines into your throat, you're probably doing okay.

How the Hell Did We Get Here?

Watch a baby breathe and you'll see their tummy go in and out with each inhale and exhale. They aren't thinking about expansion or their diaphragm or the muscles in their pelvic floor. As the mother of a one-year-old, I can say with certainty that they are not thinking about their breathing; they're thinking about finding something they shouldn't have and putting it in their mouth. Or "Baby Shark."

So how do bad breathing habits develop? I have a few theories. The first one starts the day the big yellow school bus picks you up. In addition to reading, writing, and arithmetic, the other branch of the learning tree is that sitting at a desk all day creates some really bad breathing habits. Kids spend literally hundreds of hours hunched over desks and screens. Sitting in a slumped position doesn't allow the diaphragm the space it needs to fully contract. The body can't get the oxygen it needs, so it turns to its backup breathing muscles in the neck and chest.

Emma Ferris, a clinical physiotherapist and creator of the Breath Effect, talks about these phenomena in her blog. Ferris says that sitting slumped over for extended periods of time can not only wreak havoc on the neck muscles, which are not designed to be active for the seventeen thousand breaths we take each day, but it's also been linked to feelings of sadness and anxiety.[13]

A whole book could be written on the link between putting kids in desks and their mental and emotional well-being, but for this book, let me just say that when it comes to breathing, bad habits often start seated at a schoolroom desk, and the negative effects last into adulthood.

Theory number two is something that has been preventing women from taking natural, full breaths since its invention in 1600 BCE. Any guesses? That's right, it's shapewear. From corsets to girdles to Spanx, the fashion industry has been waging war on women's natural bodies, and natural breathing patterns, since before the time of Christ.[14]

Let me be clear, I am not anti-shapewear. Post–baby number two, I credit shapewear with my ability to wear three-quarters of my current wardrobe. I'm all for feeling confident, and if the smoothing effect from a pair of Spanx makes you feel more like the goddess that you are—or just makes you feel more comfortable in your favorite dress—then who am I to judge? I do, however, want to caution you that wearing overly tight shapewear can cause breathing problems and even lead to digestive issues like acid reflux.[15]

A few years ago, I accompanied my husband to his office's holiday party. The party started at a wine bar and then moved to a fancy hotel, which his company had rented out completely for the event. It was his first year with the company and would be my first time meeting many of his colleagues. I wanted to dress to impress.

I bought a sexy black cocktail dress with lace sleeves, a low-cut V-neck, and a tight-fitting bodice. I've always been a little soft in the middle, so I also bought a waist trainer. If you're unfamiliar with waist trainers, they're basically corsets that either zip or use hook-and-eye closures rather than laces. This particular waist trainer was endorsed by Kim K, so it was the obvious choice.

I used the size guide and took my measurements before ordering, but when the waist trainer arrived, it was definitely smaller than expected. How it was going to fit around all of me, or more precisely, how I was going to get it to fit around all of me, remained a mystery—one I decided to wait to solve until absolutely necessary, hoping in the meantime that my "New Relative" alerts on 23andMe would turn up a wealthy British fourth cousin who would send one of her lady's maids from across the pond to assist me Downton Abbey style.

On the day of the party, with no lady's maid in sight, I ended up laying down on my closet floor with the waist trainer underneath me and then pulling it closed, one painful eye hook at a time, while simultaneously holding my breath and wriggling from side to side like a slowly dying cockroach. Hearing his owner in obvious peril, the dog joined me, so when my husband came upstairs to see if I was ready to leave, he found me naked on my closet floor, my torso half encased in magenta-colored rubber, and our German shepherd standing over me, extremely concerned and panting heavily.

The moral of this story is that if you're going to order a waist trainer, size up. The other moral is that even though I eventually got the waist trainer on and it did give me Kim K–style curves, it also prevented me from sitting, eating, and drinking anything carbonated, even though champagne is my absolute favorite adult beverage and they were serving Moët. When the night ended, I sprinted to the parking garage, unzipped my dress, ripped the waist trainer off, and immediately typed Taco Bell into the GPS.

My final theory, after working with literally thousands of women in my career, is that women are terrified of taking up too much space. That's right: Women are scared of being large. I'm not referring to body weight. I know plenty of single-digit pant size women who are just as afraid to take up space as us double-digit mamas. What I'm referring to is the fear of release. Releasing breath. Releasing tension. Releasing the thoughts and opinions you've been stockpiling in your brain's storage unit but are too afraid to actually share. Releasing the conversations you know you need to have but are too afraid to start. Releasing your goals and dreams into the world for all to see and hear.

Holding all that inside is exhausting. I'm exhausted just writing about it. Instead of spending your time and energy trying to keep your voice hidden, what if you allowed your body to release it? What if you were able to flip the switch from a life of chaos to a life of calm? What if you stopped sucking it in and squeezing it down and instead allowed your breath to relax your body and energize your voice? The possibilities are endless.

Summary

- The breath is the most important tool you have when speaking. Breath relaxes the body and energizes the voice. It also allows you to gather your thoughts, get back on track if you've gotten off, and better control the conversation.
- Inadequate breath support, or not having enough air, can show up as heavy breathing or gasping for air while speaking; tension in the chest, neck, and shoulders; a lack of volume, particularly at the ends of phrases; and a lack of energy in the voice. It also increases anxiety.
- Your lungs are covered with nerves that connect to the autonomic nervous system, and most of the connections to the parasympathetic system are on the lower parts of the lobes. Deep breathing activates the parasympathetic nervous system and helps you calm down. The slower and deeper your breathing, the more powerful the parasympathetic nervous system's response is and the calmer you become.
- Living in a heightened state of anxiety may also mean you're living in a state of chronic hyperventilation. If you believe you have some dysfunctional breathing habits, breath work, such as holding your breath to become more

comfortable with slightly rising CO_2 levels and rectangle breathing, may help.

- "Diaphragmatic breathing" and "belly breathing" are just super-sexy terms for breathing naturally, when your belly is allowed to go in and out. To be clear, you are always breathing into and out of your lungs.
- The body naturally expands in three places when you breathe: the chest, abdomen, and pelvic floor. Every body is different, so every body is going to expand a bit differently. As long as you aren't wearing your shoulders as earrings and constantly holding your belly muscles in tightly, you're probably doing okay.
- Sitting in a slumped position, whether at a desk or looking at your phone, prohibits the diaphragm from expanding and activates secondary breathing muscles in the neck, which, over time, may lead to neck pain. Studies have shown sitting in this position also leads to feelings of anxiety and sadness.
- Regularly wearing overly tight clothing, like shapewear, impedes the body's ability to breathe naturally and may also cause digestive issues, like acid reflux.
- Take. Up. Space. With your breath, your body, and your voice. Like the Chicks said, "She needs wide open spaces."[16]

Chapter 3

The Power of Posture

From the time I was two until early high school, I took ballet lessons. Twice a week I put on my pink tights and black leotard and my dad dropped me off at Miss Janine's School of Dance, a small-town studio run by Miss Janine, a fifty-something former prima ballerina with tightly curled brown hair and a thick German accent. I'd point my toes, raise my arms, and tremble in fear when Miss Janine herself descended from her upstairs office, dance pants softly swishing, and stand quietly in the corner of the room . . . judging.

When Miss Janine came in, our teacher would call us all to the barre so she could check our work. There are few things more terrifying for an eleven-year-old girl than trying to balance on tiptoe while a German woman with a wooden pointer and a sour expression evaluates your rapidly growing body.

"Suck in." The pointer tapped my belly. "Tuck under." The pointer tapped my behind. "Shoulders back." "Pull up," she'd say, grabbing an imaginary string from the top of my head and pulling it up toward the ceiling. I'd suck and tuck and stretch my neck like a swan, desperate for her approval, which rarely came, as my body has always been more suited to surviving the Irish potato famine than dancing gracefully *en pointe*.

Ballet at Miss Janine's was my first experience with posture. As a kid, posture wasn't something I thought about. I sat and stood and ran and jumped and slid down my pony's neck like a slide—yes, I was the little girl who wanted a pony and got one; be jealous—without giving a second thought to how my body was able to do these things or if any of them would end in injury.

As an adult, well, things are just a little bit different. I think about my posture a lot. Mostly because I read a BuzzFeed article about how looking down at your phone constantly can cause something called a "Buffalo hump," and I am terrified of getting one. I am proudly body positive: Stretch marks, cellulite, rolls—I've got them all and still (usually) think I look damn good, but even I draw the line at "Buffalo hump."

YOUR POSTURE AND YOUR VOICE

If you saw Amy Cuddy's popular TED Talk "Your Body Language May Shape Who You Are," you are already familiar with the power of posture to change how others perceive you and how you feel about yourself.[1] According to Cuddy, spending two minutes in one of her four power poses before a meeting or interview can change your body chemistry, leaving you feeling like an Amazon warrior ready for battle.[2] But did you know that your posture also affects the sound of your voice?

From chapter 1, you know that the sound your vocal folds make as air passes through them is like a duck call or the mouthpiece of a horn without the horn attached. It sounds nothing like the voice you hear coming out of your mouth. Your vocal tract—everything from the vocal folds up to and out of your mouth—shapes the sound into the words you speak. The way those words sound has everything to do with the shape of your vocal tract.

Think about a trumpet versus a tuba. Both instruments use exactly the same mouthpiece, but the sounds they make are very different. This is because their size and shape are different. When it comes to creating sound, the rule is "more space = more bass," so the tuba, being a larger instrument, has a lower sound. Your vocal tract works in the same way, except instead of a fixed space for the sound waves to bounce off, its shape can change.

Your head meets your spine at the atlanto-occipital (AO) joint. To find your AO joint, place your fingers in the small indents behind your ears and imagine drawing a line between them. In the middle is the AO joint. If you make small circles with your head, you should feel when it's freely moving and supported by the AO joint, like a bobblehead figure.

Your head is heavy. (It's at this point in my university lectures that I quote *Jerry Maguire*—"The human head weighs eight pounds"—and my students, who were born almost a decade after the movie came out, look at me blankly because they have no idea what I'm talking about. This has happened every year for the last six years, but will I stop making the joke? No, no I will not.)

Your head is heavy, so keeping it balanced on your spine, at the AO joint, allows your cervical spine to do what it's made to do, which is support your head.[3] Once the head moves out of alignment, either forward (like a turtle) or backward (like a wrestler) your neck muscles start to take over. This can cause neck pain and discomfort, and it can also change the sound of your voice.

Think back to my trumpet-versus-tuba analogy. The sound of these instruments is different, in part, because they are shaped differently. When your neck thrusts forward, you are changing the shape of your instrument (your vocal tract). In this case, you are making your vocal tract smaller, so the sound of your voice loses bass or warmth.

Shaping Your Vocal Tract

Try this with me. Thrust your head all the way forward, like a turtle; think of this as "1." Now pull your head all the way back, like a wrestler; think of this as, "10." The balance point for the head on the AO joint is around a 4, 5, or 6. Using a 1–10 scale is a great way to check in with yourself throughout the day. If that number creeps too far in one direction or the other, take a moment and adjust.

Once you've found the balance point, say the following phrase, "Hi, my name is (insert your name here)." Listen to the sound of your voice. You can record yourself if you'd like, but you don't have to. Keep saying the phrase while thrusting your head forward, toward 1 on your scale. Do you hear the sound change? Now pull your head back toward 10 on your scale. How does the sound change? Move your head slowly between 1 and 10 and listen to the difference its position makes to the sound of your voice.

You may notice that when you thrust your head forward, your voice takes on a more nasal or abrasive quality. This is because you've shrunk your vocal tract. Remember, more space equals more bass, so when you reduce the space, you also reduce the warmth in your voice. This is especially important to keep in mind when you are presenting at a podium with a microphone, talking on Zoom or the phone, and other instances when your natural posture may be altered.

Head, Shoulders, (Pelvis), Knees, and Toes

Let's talk about your shoulders next. Whether because of ballet class, my mother's continuous reminders during my middle school years, or my desire to keep my rapidly deflating tits up, when I think of posture, my shoulders are the first thing that comes to mind.

You want your shoulders to hang out underneath your ears, more down rather than back. If we use the 1–10 scale again, rounding your shoulders forward as far as they will go would be 1, and pushing them back militaristically would be 10. Again, aim for a 4, 5, or 6. The goal is for your collarbone to be parallel to the floor and your arms to hang comfortably, and symmetrically, at your sides. Pulling your shoulders back too far can actually prevent the rib cage from expanding properly when you inhale, prohibiting a natural, full breath.[4]

Connecting the upper body to the lower body are the pelvis and hips. The pelvis offers support, distributing the weight of your upper body onto your thigh bones, or femurs, when standing, and also allows for the motion of bending at the waist and rotating your legs. It's also the source of a common postural problem, the forward pelvis tilt, or swayback.[5] A swayback is when your lower back arcs too much, overlengthening the hamstrings and causing them to feel tight. Standing with a swayback can not only cause hamstring pain, it also underworks the glutes and prevents the muscles of the pelvic floor from experiencing their full range of motion, weakening them. If you want to keep your peach tight and your pants dry, pay attention to your pelvis.

Your knees are affected by what is happening above them, at the hips, and below them, at the ankles and feet. When standing, your weight should be evenly distributed among your five toes and from the ball to the heel of your foot.[6] Want to check your alignment? Take a look at the bottoms of your bare feet. The more wear and tear on an area of your foot, the thicker and denser the calluses will be. Ideally, the calluses are pretty evenly distributed between all five toes and the outside and inside of your foot. If you find that one side or the other has denser calluses, it may be time to evaluate how you're standing and the shoes you're wearing.

The Problem with Heels (I Know. I'm Sorry.)

In her blog post "The Top 5 Reasons to Stop Wearing Heels," podiatrist Dr. Joanna Shuman says that most common foot problems, from bunions to deformities to arthritis, are linked to wearing high heels.[7] Even a slight heel causes a shift in your center of gravity, creating an angled platform that your entire body now operates from.

If reading this made you depressed, I'm with you. I love heels. I love looking at them. I love trying them on. I love pairing them with a cute, slightly offbeat outfit and prancing down the sidewalk as if I'm Carrie Bradshaw on the way to meet my girlfriends for cosmos. I have an entire Pinterest board dedicated to the shoes I will buy when my scratch-off lottery ticket habit finally pays off. Never mind that I can barely walk in them, find wearing them painful, and once broke several bones in my foot as a result of rolling my ankle while running down stairs wearing a pair of platform sandals, my love endures.

So what's a girl to do? My best piece of advice is that if you're going to present or lead a meeting while standing, be absolutely sure to practice in the shoes you'll be wearing. When I auditioned for grad school, I had to sing about twenty minutes of music and then do a talk back with the voice faculty. The day before my audition, I carefully picked out my outfit: a form-fitting black dress with a colorful neck scarf that told the panel, "I'm a mature, professional, creative woman. I will work hard, be on time, and bring you a great bottle of cab on your birthday." All true. I also chose a pair of four-inch, yellow python polka-dot Dolce & Gabbana heels I purchased off eBay for $75, which I had only worn once, out to dinner, where the only walking I did was from the cab to the restaurant and back.

When it was my turn to sing, I walked confidently into the recital hall, climbed the stairs to the stage, and began my audition. Five minutes in, my feet started to hurt. Ten minutes in, my legs started shaking. I spent the rest of my audition trying to discreetly shift my weight from one foot to the other in the hopes I could relieve some of the pain—and trying not to fall down.

This all could have been avoided if I had done a dry run of my audition wearing my shoes. Either I would have determined that four-inch spiked heels were, in fact, not the best choice to wear when standing for forty-five minutes on a wooden stage, or . . . actually, there is no "or." I would have chosen other shoes. If you're going to be standing and talking for any decent length of time, for the love of Jimmy Choo, practice in your shoes.

Posture Self-Assessments

The Mirror Test

Stand facing a full-length mirror. Look to see if:

- Your shoulders are level and beneath the ears
- Your head is straight, not tilting to one side or the other
- The space between your arms and torso is equal on both sides
- Your hips are level and your kneecaps face straight ahead
- Your pelvis feels neutral, not swayed back or tucked under
- Your ankles are straight
- Your feet are straight forward and your weight feels evenly distributed on all five toes and from ball of the foot to heel

Stand sideways in front of a full-length mirror. Look (or have a partner look) to see if:

- Your head is erect, not thrust forward or pulled back
- Your chin is parallel to the floor, not tilted up or down
- Your shoulders are in line with your ears, not pulled back or rounded forward
- Your stomach is neutral, neither pulled in rigidly nor pushed out
- Your knees are straight
- Your lower back has a slight forward curve and your pelvis is not swayed back or tucked under

The Wall Test

Stand with the back of your head, shoulders, and butt touching the wall and your heels six inches from the baseboard.

- Use your hand to check the distance between your neck and the wall.
- If your head, shoulders, or butt cannot touch the wall, or if you can slide more than three fingers behind your neck, you may have a posture issue that is affecting your health in some capacity.

The Floor Angel

Lie on the floor with your knees bent, feet flat on the floor, lower rib cage in contact with the floor, and arms out to the sides in a 90-degree "field goal" position. Keep the back of your head on the floor and your chin tucked in. Maintain the following positions for thirty seconds:

- Raise your hips off the floor.
- Raise your rib cage off the floor.
- Maintain head contact with the floor.
- Maintain wrist and arm contact with the floor.

If you cannot maintain any of these positions, your posture needs work. No worries! The following pages contain stretches and exercises to help correct posture issues.

Five Stretches for Better Posture

If you've taken a yoga class of any kind, you're probably familiar with the following five stretches. What you may not be aware of is the positive impact they can have on your posture and alignment. Architects and designers often refer to the concept of "tensegrity." Tensegrity equals tension plus integrity.[8] The term was coined to describe structures that are held together by the balance of tension members, not compression. Most of the structures we see depend on compression to hold them together: brick on top of brick. While you may think of your body this way—head, shoulders, knees, and toes, one atop the other—in reality our bones float in a sea of soft tissue. The tissue pulls continuously inward, while the bones resist outward. The resulting tension is what gives our body its structure.

If you pile snow on one corner of a roof, eventually that corner will cave in. This is what happens with compression structures: The most strained part fails. With tensegrity structures, like your body, the strain is distributed throughout the structure, so instead of the strained part failing, the weakest part of the overall structure fails. When one part of the body is improperly aligned, the effects can be felt throughout the entire body. This is why pain in the lower back can be the result of a problem in the shoulder or ankle. Pain in the left hip can also be the result of attending a '90s throwback party and forgetting that you're not, in fact, twenty-two anymore. (Old Lady Doyle-Mekkes can't drop it as hot as she used to.)

The following five stretches work to stretch, strengthen, and move the body's balance points: your neck, shoulders, spine, hips, pelvis, knees, and ankles. Poor posture, stiffness, and pain often show up in these areas, so taking time daily to move and stretch them out is important. If you think you don't have time, just remember: Buffalo humps are real, and they're coming for you.

Child's Pose

How to Do It

- Start on your hands and knees.
- Take your knees shoulder-width apart.
- Keeping the tops of your feet on the floor, bring your big toes together.
- Walk your hands forward, either extending your arms straight or draping your arms on the floor alongside your body.
- Slowly lower your hips back so they rest on top of your heels.

- Lower your forehead to the floor.
- Stay here for five to ten deep breaths.

Why It Works

Child's Pose is great if you tend to slouch, because it lengthens and stretches your spine, and if you stretch your arms over your head, it encourages motion in your shoulders.

Cat-Cow

How to Do It

- Start on all fours. Keep your elbows under your shoulders, wrists under elbows. Spread your fingers wide for added stability. Keep your knees directly under your hips and the tops of your feet flat on the floor.
- To find your starting position, keep your neck neutral so you're looking down at a spot a few inches in front of your fingers and lengthening your spine from your tailbone to your head.
- Begin with Cat: Exhale and tuck your tailbone under. Use your belly muscles to push your spine toward the ceiling, creating the shape of a startled cat with its back up. Keep your neck long while you reach your head toward your chest.
- Inhale, and on your next exhale, reverse the position into Cow: Lift your chin and chest and look up at the ceiling while you draw your shoulders away from your ears, pushing your belly down toward the floor.
- Cycle through the Cat-Cow movements five to ten times.
- You can also do this exercise standing: With feet shoulder width apart, place your hands on your thighs, then repeat the motion of Cat-Cow, moving your spine, neck, and head as you did when on all fours.

Why It Works

Swayback, tucked-under pelvis, slouching, and neck thrusting all have to do with spinal awareness—or the lack thereof. Cat-Cow requires you to pay attention to your spine as it moves, increasing spinal awareness. When done standing, it increases your awareness of how your spine moves in relation to the rest of your body. Kneeling or standing, Cat-Cow is a great way to stretch your spine if you've been sitting for long periods of time.

Downward-Facing Dog

How to Do It

- Begin on all fours.
- Tuck your toes under and lift your hips up toward the ceiling.
- Reach or walk your heels back so you feel a stretch in your calf muscles, but not so far that your feet are flat on the ground.
- Release your head and let it drop toward the floor like a rag doll.
- Keep your hands and wrists parallel and facing forward. Don't scrunch your shoulders up toward your ears.
- Stay here and breathe for five to ten deep breaths.
- If the position becomes uncomfortable, relax back into Child's Pose, and try again when you're ready.

Why It Works

Excess time spent at a desk working on a computer can leave your shoulders and chest rounded forward. Downward-Facing Dog helps to open the anterior chest wall and shoulders, which may relieve neck and back pain and help you sit taller.

Plank

How to Do It

- Start on all fours with your fingers spread. You may also start on your knees and elbows.
- Step your feet back, one at a time, keeping your core muscles active and your pelvis neutral. Don't let your hips sag toward the floor or rise toward the ceiling.
- Pull up from your kneecaps with your quads. Activate your calves by pressing back through your heels.
- Don't let your shoulders creep up to your ears. Stretch your neck and imagine your shoulder blades pulling away from each other.
- Do four to six rounds of ten deep inhales and exhales.

Why It Works

Core strength is vital for good posture. Plank strengthens your belly muscles and brings awareness to your spine and pelvis so you can become more mindful about swayback or your pelvis being tucked under.

Spine Rotation

How to Do It

- Start on all fours, with your fingers spread apart slightly.
- Put your left hand behind your head while keeping your right hand on the ground in front of you.
- On an exhale, rotate your left elbow to the ceiling. Hold for a deep breath in and out, and feel the stretch in the front of your torso.
- Return to your starting position. Repeat for five to ten breaths.
- Switch arms and repeat.

Why It Works

Rotating your spine improves flexibility and mobility in your thoracic spine (the middle and upper back). It loosens tight back muscles and may help reduce stiffness in your lower back.

If you find you have persistent posture issues or are concerned about pain due to misalignment, make an appointment with your physician or a physical therapist.

POSTURE AND EMOTIONS

Your posture not only affects your body physically, it also conveys how you're feeling to those around you.[9] We often think of conveying emotions through facial expressions and tone of voice, but a rapidly growing field of research points to body posture as being equally, if not more, important in alerting others to how you're feeling on the inside.[10]

I want to tell you the true story of how a friend of mine landed a high-paying job with neither experience in the industry nor the proper education. (To be clear, I do not condone this approach, I am simply using this as an example of the power of posture.)

For two years when I was starting out as a performer, I worked for a theatre company in South Korea. Living in Seoul, one of the first things I learned was that the Korean people love to dress to impress. In the center of Seoul is Mount Namsan, an 860-foot peak with a park and trails winding to the top, where there's an observatory and snacks. It's an easy climb, the trails are paved, and you can comfortably hike to the top wearing a casual outfit and tennis shoes. Climbing Namsan, it was common to see groups of Korean hikers dressed as if they were ready to scale Everest instead of strolling uphill to an awaiting ice cream truck and a pretty view of the city. I'm talking fully color-coordinated, layered hiking apparel, matching CamelBak, aluminum trekking poles, and occasionally a sherpa (kidding). Whatever Mount Namsan had in store, they were ready for it.

The same thing happened at the golf course near my apartment, where the fairways were filled with golfers who looked more like they were headed for Augusta National than the next hole on a par-3 course sandwiched between a high-rise apartment complex and an IKEA. It didn't matter if there were only four clubs in their miniature-sized golf bags; those clubs were going to be TaylorMade and come with a headcover that matched the golfer's outfit.

My friend, who also worked at the theatre company, finished her contract and moved to Los Angeles, where she waited tables and did temp jobs between film auditions. She wasn't making great money, especially in a city where rent for a single bedroom in a house in the valley where the landlord did black-market Botox injections and lip fillers out of the garage and limited A/C usage to four hours per day was topping $900 a month circa 2008.

Scrolling the job sites one day, she came across a posting for a job at a Korean company that paid really well and appeared to require little more than the ability to source Korean products on the internet for this company to sell and an MBA. Online shopping skills: check; MBA . . . not so much. So what did she do? She went to Saks and bought a killer suit on credit (she could pay it off once she landed her new fat paycheck), got a blowout, threw her shoulders back, strutted into that company like she owned the place, and asked to speak to the manager.

She stood with her feet wide and her head high, taking up every inch of space she could in that reception area. Everything from the tip of her head to the point of her Manolos looked like "success." She got the job.

My point in telling you this story is not to encourage you to immediately go out and spend hundreds of dollars on new clothes to swindle your way into a job you're not qualified for; my point is that how you carry yourself says a whole lot about who you are and how you're feeling.

Posture and Confidence

According to a research study out of Ohio State University, sitting or standing up straight makes you more confident in your own skills and knowledge. Seventy-one university students came into a classroom where they were told they'd be simultaneously participating in two studies: one for the business school and one for the school of the arts. The students were told the arts study was on a person's ability to maintain a specific posture while doing other activities. They were then told to either sit up straight or slouch and, while maintaining that posture, complete an evaluation on how well they would do as a working professional.

The results were shocking. Almost unanimously, the students who sat up straight rated their potential for professional success as high, while the students who slouched did the opposite. Richard Petty, coauthor of the study and professor of psychology at OSU, was clear that the students never heard the words "confidence" or "doubt." They had no idea what the study was about or what their assigned body postures had to do with it.

In an article on the study for *Science Daily*, Petty said, "People assume their confidence is coming from their own thoughts. They don't realize their posture is affecting how much they believe in what they're thinking. If they did realize that, posture wouldn't have such an effect."[11]

Quick Posture Checklist

We've already gone through creating proper posture in detail, so here's a quick checklist for everyday use. Remember, you can think of posture on a 1–10 scale, with 1 and 10 being the extremes of misalignment. Strive to stay around a 4, 5, or 6.

- Chin parallel to the floor, head centered on spine
- Shoulders even and below ears (think down, not back)
- Neutral spine and hips (watch your pelvis, Elvis)

- Abdominal muscles activated but not rigid
- Knees even and pointing straight ahead, not locked back
- All five toes on the floor, weight centered between the ball and heel of the foot

Monday Morning Reset

Here's a series of stretches and exercises I give my students on Monday mornings to help get their brains, bodies, and voices prepared for the day and week ahead. It combines a little breath work, posture and alignment, and even some self-massage focused on waking up the muscles of the face and voice. I highly recommend using it on Mondays—and any other day you need to realign and refocus.

Begin by standing with feet shoulder width apart, arms at your sides. Close your eyes and take a couple of deep breaths, in through the nose and out on a "shhhh" (like a leaky tire). Try to clear your mind and turn your focus inward.

When you're ready, open your eyes, reach your arms high above your head, and look up at the ceiling. On an exhale, bend at the waist and take your hands toward the floor. Go ahead and keep a bend in your knees if you need to; this is not meant to be a serious hamstring stretch. Hang loosely, like a rag doll, and breathe. On each inhale, reach forward out of your pelvis, and on the exhale, see if you can let your body hang a bit closer to the floor.

Grab your elbows and gently pull down toward the floor. Breathe. Shake your body loosely from side to side. This is usually when I feel a super satisfying release in my spine. Release your elbows and let your hands fall back to the floor. Slowly nod your head "yes," then shake your head "no." Be sure your neck muscles aren't holding your head up; let it fall freely toward the floor.

When you're ready, inhale and start to roll up through the spine, maintaining a slight bend in the knees. Only roll as far as a single inhale will take you, then exhale. Repeat this until you are back to standing. Once you're standing, scan through your body and check your alignment.

Next, take your fingers and gently massage your temples. The temporalis muscle, which contracts when you clench your jaw, connects at the temples, so they're a great massage point to release tension. Temple massage can also be helpful for soothing a headache. When you're ready, move your fingers down to your temporomandibular joint (TMJ). That's the horseshoe-shaped joint located in front of your ears. If you grind your teeth at night you may be familiar with this joint. Gentle self-massage can help relieve jaw tension and pain. Finally, with your palms flat, place the tips of your fingers underneath your cheekbones, then open and close your mouth. Adjust the pressure of your fingers so it feels good to you. For more pressure, you can also use your knuckles.

Tilt your head toward your right shoulder and use your left hand to find the large, ropy muscle that runs down the right side of your neck, the sternocleidomastoid (SCM). The SCM is used when turning the head. Neck sore after sleeping? It's probably your SCM. Using your thumb and index finger like a pincher claw, grab the SCM and gently massage it from its top, near the base of your skull, to its bottom, near your collarbone. Tilt your head to the left and repeat using your right hand.

When you're finished with your SCM massage, tilt your head again to the right and reach toward the floor with your left hand, like a small child is pulling on your hand, to stretch out the side of your neck and top of the shoulder. Keep the stretch and turn your chin down toward your armpit (stink check) to feel a stretch along the back of the neck. Repeat on the opposite side.

If it feels good to you, take your hands on either side of your larynx, at the front of your neck. For some people, this can cause nausea or an icky feeling of touching an internal structure you don't normally come into contact with. If that's you, just skip this.

If you're comfortable, take your hands and gently massage up and down the front of your throat. Gently move the larynx side to side. This is also a great way to get phlegm off of your vocal folds. You might notice you can now swallow the gunk that was making you cough or want to clear your throat constantly.

The whole reset usually takes me about five to ten minutes, but take as little or as much time as you need. On some days, certain areas of your face and neck might need more time than others, and that's okay. If any part of this reset feels uncomfortable to you, feel free to skip it or substitute a favorite stretch of your own.

SUMMARY

- Posture affects the sound of your voice. Your head meets your spine at the atlanto-occipital joint, where its weight is supported by the cervical spine. Thrusting your head forward (like a turtle) or pulling it back (like a wrestler) changes the shape of your vocal tract and may make your voice take on a nasal or abrasive quality.
- Posture affects your breathing. Your shoulders should hang out under your ears, more down than back, with your collarbone parallel to the floor. Taking your shoulders too far back, in a militaristic stance, impedes rib cage movement and prevents the lungs from fully expanding.
- A common postural problem is the swayback, tilting your pelvis backward and thrusting your belly forward, so your hips are behind rather than underneath your body. Standing with a swayback overstretches the hamstrings, underworks the glutes, and prevents the muscles of your pelvic floor from going through their full range of motion, weakening them. If you want to keep your peach tight and your pants dry, pay attention to your pelvis.
- You can tell how you are distributing your weight on your feet by looking at the calluses on your soles. You want the

calluses to be evenly distributed and of even thickness. Wearing a heeled shoe, even a low heel, changes your body's center of gravity and takes you out of alignment. Save your heels for the days when you'll be seated, and if you are going to stand while presenting, be sure to practice in the shoes you'll be wearing.

- Think of each part of your body's alignment as existing on a scale of 1 to 10, with 1 and 10 being the farthest from neutral. Try to keep your head, shoulders, hips, knees, and feet near a 4, 5, or 6 on your scale.
- Your posture affects how others perceive you and how you perceive yourself. Studies show that maintaining correct posture makes you more confident in your own abilities and knowledge.
- Stretches, self-massage, and exercises can all help to correct postural and alignment problems. If postural problems persist, it's a good idea to see your doctor or a physical therapist for further evaluation.

Chapter 4

The Nitty Gritty

Common Challenges Facing Women's Voices and How to Fix Them

Since you're reading this book, I'm guessing there is something about your voice you're not happy with. Whether this unhappiness is part of your current reality or the result of something or someone in your past, it's time for her to pack her bags and move on. You have things to do, people to see, and lives to change—including your own.

If you already have an idea of what your vocal challenges are, great. Maybe you've received feedback that you speak too quickly, too quietly, or without confidence. If so, you're totally in the right place. If you aren't sure of the specifics or are brand-new to using your voice beyond day-to-day conversations, great—you're also totally in the right place. If you're a pretty confident speaker and just want a tune-up before an upcoming event . . . you guessed it—this is the place for that too.

First, you need to see and hear what your audience is seeing and hearing, so grab your cell phone and record a video using one of the short scripts below. Record yourself (yes, video on) with the goal of re-creating how you normally speak. If you sit at work answering the phone or are preparing for a meeting or interview, then sit. If you normally stand while talking to clients or patients or are preparing for a speech or presentation, then stand. Don't overthink it. This is simply to find your starting point.

The voice you hear and the voice your audience hears will always be two different things. If you've ever listened to yourself on a recording and thought, "I do not sound like that," you know what I'm talking about. (And yes, you do.)

When you speak, you create vibrations in the bones of your head, these vibrations have sound, and that sound travels to your eardrums via a process called bone conduction.[1] So not only are you hearing the sound coming out of your mouth, you're also hearing all the additional sound these vibrations create. Your audience is only hearing what's coming out of your mouth, and like it or not, that's all that matters.

Watch the video using the Self-Evaluation Worksheet for guidance. What do you see? What do you hear? How does it make you feel? Try to review the video as your audience might, rather than as yourself—so none of that negative "I look fat . . . this is awful . . . when did I last dye my roots?" shit.

Is your voice stable or does it waver? Are you too loud? Too quiet? Is your voice breathy or clear? Is the pitch of your voice too high? Too low? Do you speak with energy and enthusiasm or authority (if that's your goal)? Do your words sound lackluster and timid? Would you hire, invest, promote, say "yes" to you?

Once you have an idea of where you're starting from, use the rest of this chapter to meet (and greet) those challenges head on. I've given you my favorite tips, tricks, and exercises created over a fifteen-plus-year career working with thousands of voices to help you create a voice that is strong, healthy, and authentically yours.

Practice Scripts

From *Little Women*, by Louisa May Alcott

> You'll get over this after awhile, and find some lovely, accomplished girl who will adore you and make a fine mistress for

your fine house. I shouldn't. I'm homely, and awkward, and odd, and old, and you'd be ashamed of me, and we should quarrel—we can't help it even now you see—and I shouldn't like elegant society and you would, and you'd hate my scribbling and I couldn't get on without it, and we should be unhappy and wish we hadn't done it and everything would be horrid.[2]

From *The Secret Garden*, by Frances Hodgson Burnett

I don't know its name, so I call it Magic. I have never seen the sun rise but Mary and Dickon have and from what they tell me I am sure that it is Magic too. Something pushes it up and draws it. Sometimes since I've been in the garden I've looked up through the trees at the sky and I have had the strange feeling of being happy as if something were pushing and drawing in my chest and making me breathe fast. Magic is always pushing and drawing and making things out of nothing. Everything is made out of Magic, leaves and trees, flowers and birds, badgers and foxes and squirrels and people.[3]

From *Pygmalion*, by George Bernard Shaw

Your calling me Miss Doolittle that day when I first came to Wimpole Street. That was the beginning of self-respect for me. And there were a hundred little things you never noticed, because they came naturally to you. Things about standing up and taking off your hat and opening doors. . . . You see, really and truly, apart from the things anyone can pick up (the dressing and the proper way of speaking, and so on), the difference between a lady and a flower girl is not how she behaves, but how she's treated. I shall always be a flower girl to Professor Higgins, because he always treats me as a flower girl, and always

> will; but I know I can be a lady to you, because you always treat me as a lady, and always will.[4]

Self-Evaluation Worksheet

Review your video recording and listen for the common vocal challenges on the list below. Number a piece of paper 1–8 and place an X next to each number that corresponds with what you hear each time you hear it. So if you find yourself mumbling once during your reading, you'd write one X; if you find yourself mumbling three times, write three X's. Then look to see which categories have the most X's. These are your top vocal challenges. Once you've identified your top challenges read the corresponding section(s) below to find my top tips, exercises, and quick fixes to each.

1. Quiet and Meek
2. Loud and Aggressive
3. Too Fast to Understand
4. Slow/Mumbled
5. Breathy
6. Croaky/Gravelly
7. Pitch Goes Up at the End of Phrases (Upspeaking)
8. Pitch Is High and Whiny

Sounding Too Meek or Too Aggressive

Speak too quietly and you're timid, lack authority, or don't know what you're talking about. Speak too loudly and you're shrill, overly emotional, dramatic, or just a bitch. There's a reason female politicians are often coached to lower their voices. Stereotypes about what constitutes authority and what power and credibility look like exist, and the benchmark for success is often very white and very male.[5]

Not only do women have to combat these stereotypes, they also often have to speak using equipment that was created for men. Most lecture halls and boardrooms use directional microphones, which pick up sound from—you guessed it!—one direction. These microphones are better at picking up lower frequencies, or lower-pitched sounds, meaning they are actually designed to make lower voices louder and higher voices softer.[6]

If that pisses you off (and it should), get this: In the 1920s, when radio technology was all the rage, Congress put a limit on the bandwidth allotted to each radio station. As a result, stations limited their signals to the bare minimum frequency thought to be needed to transmit speech.[7] Basically, Dick and Harry got together and decided that the only voices worth hearing on the radio were theirs, so they limited the sounds that could be successfully transported into America's living rooms.

Shocking, right? I didn't think so, either. What is shocking, and really disappointing, is that in the last hundred years, things haven't changed all that much. In an article for the *New Yorker*, temporal media artist, engineer, historian, and educator Tina Tallon writes, "Even today, many data-compression algorithms and bluetooth speakers disproportionately affect high frequencies and consonants, and women's voices lose definition, sounding thin and tinny."[8]

Rather than change a system that was literally created to silence the voices of half the world's population, women are simply told to lower their pitch. Speaking in a voice that isn't authentically yours? I don't think so. Instead, try these suggestions:

- Advocate for yourself. If you're going to be speaking at an event with a large audience and using amplification, see if there's an audio engineer assigned to the venue and check in with her before your speech, especially if you are one of multiple speakers. If you are following a man with a loud, booming voice, she may need to adjust the equalizer before you begin to ensure your voice is heard clearly.

- Don't be afraid to move the microphone or adjust its height. Also, don't be afraid to ask for a mic if one isn't provided but you feel it would be helpful. Remember, directional mics pick up only the sound that is directly in front of them, and the closer to the mic you are, the fuller your voice will sound. If you're going to be walking and talking or using a handheld mic, be sure to practice! Grab a spoon, kitchen karaoke style, and practice keeping it near your mouth while you speak.

How to Speak Louder (While Still Sounding Like You)

If you're going to be speaking without a mic and being heard while still sounding like yourself is a concern, here are a few exercises you can use to safely and healthily increase your volume.

Speak Louder (Really)

When a client listens back to her voice recording and complains about not being loud enough, my first question is, "Can you speak louder?" (That's why they pay me the big bucks.) It may seem silly, but if you're used to speaking softly or you aren't aware of how softly you've been speaking, sometimes all you need is permission to be louder. To be clear: You don't need my, or anyone else's, permission to get loud (okay, maybe JLo's), but sometimes you do need a reminder.

Create Resonance

You now know that when you speak, air passes through your vocal folds, setting them into motion. (If this concept is a new one to you, go back and read chapter 1.) The sound then gets shaped by three main chambers: your pharynx (back of the throat), your mouth, and your nose. When these chambers get excited and amplify the sound, we call it resonance. Basically, resonance is using your air to get louder, rather than just your muscles. Resonance is how opera singers can still be heard up in the nosebleeds even though they're not wearing mics. It's also how you can increase your volume without yelling.

It's Such a Good Vibration

Before you begin this exercise, start a voice recording (a voice memo on your phone is fine) and read the following Audrey Hepburn quote:

> I believe in being strong when everything seems to be going wrong. I believe that happy girls are the prettiest girls. I believe that tomorrow is another day, and I believe in miracles.[9]

Don't overthink it, just read it a few times in your normal, everyday voice.

Now, say, "Mhmm," as if you are agreeing with someone. Say it again, but this time keep humming, "Mhmmmmmmmmmm." Focus on the buzz in your mouth and the front of your face: the space behind your upper lip, your front teeth, and wherever else you feel it.

Continue to hum, breathing whenever you need to. Get louder, then softer, and see if you can maintain that buzz. Once you feel comfortable with maintaining the buzz, hum loudly and then speak in a monotone (all on one pitch, like a robot):

> Mary Moon makes magnificent mojitos.

Speak the line a few more times, still monotone, and see how much buzz you can create. (More mojitos equals more buzz, am

I right?) Finally, hum and then speak the line naturally, allowing the pitch to move up and down as it usually does.

Start a new voice memo, and record the first phrase again:

> I believe in being strong when everything seems to be going wrong. I believe that happy girls are the prettiest girls. I believe that tomorrow is another day, and I believe in miracles.

Do you hear a difference? My goal through resonant voice work (which is a fancy name for what you're doing) is that your voice becomes clearer and more energized, and that you are more easily able to fill a room with sound without yelling.

Vocal Fry: Everything's a Kardashian (and I'm Not Mad about It)

If you've watched a show, interview, or reel with one of the Kardashian sisters in it, you've no doubt heard the throaty way they often speak. (And if you haven't, where have you been?) This low, creaky sound is called vocal fry.[10] Historically, vocal fry was considered to be a voice disorder; however, it has steadily crept into American speech, beginning with California surfer culture in the 1960s.[11]

Vocal fry is speaking from the lowest part, or register, of your voice. Contrary to popular belief, vocal fry isn't inherently bad for your voice; there's very little research indicating that vocal fry causes vocal injury.[12] However, a quick Google search results in a slew of articles from blogs to magazines to academic journals about the harm vocal fry is doing to women's voices.

Why? Well, the general consensus seems to be that vocal fry makes women sound less competent, less educated, less attractive, and less hirable.[13] Let's break that down for a moment, using Kim K as our test subject.

Less competent and educated? Well, Kim has founded thirteen businesses; her most successful undertaking, the shapewear brand SKIMS, is currently a multibillion-dollar brand available worldwide.[14] On her fourth attempt, she passed California's "baby bar," a first-year law school exam with a pass rate among traditional law students of about 20 percent, and she's lobbied for criminal justice reform.[15] Seems pretty competent and educated to me.

Even if you're not a fan, it's hard to argue that Kim isn't attractive. As for hirable, is there a brand that doesn't want her on board? I could make similar arguments for actress Zooey Deschanel and singer Katy Perry, who also speak with vocal fry.[16] What gives?

In their article for the feminist philosophy journal *Hypatia*, about understanding the negative reactions to female vocal fry, Monika Chao and Julia R. S. Bursten use the term "non-content-based response."[17] Say a woman comments that it's windy outside. A content-based response might be, "Yes, it is," "Hold onto your hat!" or "I heard it might get up to 50 mph." A non-content-based response might be, "Shhh; quiet down." "TGIF, am I right?" or "There's a wolf behind you!" Non-content-based responses don't respond to *what* was said but rather only that *something* was said.[18]

Non-content-based responses pause the conversation. If you said, "Wow it's windy today," and the response was, "Shh! There's a wolf behind you," now you have to question if there really is a wolf, if it's going to attack, and how to get away. More importantly, you must consider whether this wolf is a werewolf, and if so, will it be turning into Taylor Lautner. You also have to decide whether to restart your conversation about the wind, which might seem unimportant now.

Non-content-based responses are silencing.[19] This may not be a big deal during a casual conversation about the wind, but it's a really big deal in high-stakes conversation. Research tells us that vocal fry elicits a negative non-content-based response.

> *Emily (speaking with vocal fry):* As you can see Mr. President, the drug trial I led was successful and we've cured cancer.
>
> *Mr. President:* Have you considered raising the pitch of your speaking voice; it's rather annoying. And you should smile more!

It may be that the older generation sees vocal fry as a "fashion trend."[20] Or it may be that lower-pitched voices sound more masculine and are perceived as stronger and more dominant, threatening the fragile egos of the patriarchy.[21]

Here's the thing: We are living in an age of female empowerment. Women aren't trying to get through the door anymore. We're through. We have a seat at the table; we've built our own tables. We're directing national intelligence and the World Trade Organization. We're throwing yellow flags at the Super Bowl and Yurchenko double pikes on the vault. We know we have the power to crush industry titans who tried to intimidate us with threats, blacklists, and office doors that automatically lock. And we know we can do it all wearing whatever the hell we want because our value and right to safety have absolutely nothing to do with our bodies and the way in which we dress them.

Our voices must reflect this power. Perhaps it isn't merely coincidence that society deems a popular vocal characteristic belonging to the most empowered generation of women ever "annoying" and "unprofessional." I'd guess sticking one's fingers in one's ears and yelling, "I can't hear you," wouldn't go over so well, so calling the speaker "annoying" seems like the logical next step. I'll ask my five-year-old to confirm.

Just Emotions Taking Me Over

How you feel has a direct effect on how you sound. Emotions play a large part in creating timbre, or the sound quality of your voice. Once you know how different emotions affect the sound of your voice, you can use each emotion as a tool to change your sound. Let's explore this. Before you begin, be sure to turn on a voice memo so you can review your results.

Begin by saying, "Hi, how are you?" in your normal, everyday speaking voice. Then say the phrase again as if you are:

- Happy (puppies and candy canes)
- Angry (someone stole your parking space, again)
- Sad (you had a no good, really bad day)
- Annoyed (channel your teen angst years)
- Normal (again, in your everyday voice)

Listen back and note the differences in your voice. Which greeting sounds most confident? Which sounds uncertain? How you feel makes a *huge* difference in how you sound. It also makes a huge difference in how others respond to what you're saying.

For extra credit, ask a few other people to listen to the recordings and give you their thoughts. Which version of your greeting makes them want to continue the conversation? Which makes them want to smile uncomfortably while slowly backing out of the room?

Take what you (and others) have observed and apply it in real life. If puppies and candy canes are the key to sounding confident and inviting, then think happy thoughts, Wendy! If a bit of anger gives your voice the edge of authority you're looking for, then get pissed! I actually love having my students sing angry because when we're angry we get louder and clearer, with better enunciation, as we attempt to make our point.

Explore other emotions as well. Humans are really good at detecting nuanced emotional tones; we can hear the difference between compassion, interest, and embarrassment.[22] We can hear when something is wrong, when someone is tired, or when someone is nervous, because their mood physically affects their voice. A study out of Yale University revealed that we can actually hear emotions in someone's voice better than we can see them on their face.[23]

Pace Yourself

Another way to up the confidence factor when speaking is to pay attention to your pace. According to a study out of the University of Michigan, the key to getting, and keeping, your listener's attention is speaking at a moderate pace, about 3.5 words per second, rather than too quickly or too slowly.[24]

This is something I struggle with. When I get excited, my pitch goes up and my words go faster. This is equally true when I drink. The vodka sodas start flowing and suddenly I'm rapping *Hamilton* lyrics at a pitch only dogs can hear. This is usually when the DJ broadcasts, "Don, it's time to come get your girl," and my husband has to escort me off the dance floor because it's 7:30 and people are trying to finish their dinners.

If you need a reminder, watch your self-evaluation video again and evaluate your pace. If you're speeding through the words or speaking so slowly that you've stopped listening and started bird watching, adjust accordingly.

Also, take note of your pauses. It's okay to pause. Pauses are a natural part of conversation. A great place to pause when speaking is wherever there would be punctuation if you were writing. Try not to pause in the middle of a word, a thought, or so many times your audience becomes confused about the content of your conversation or concerned for your health.

Other Habits to Break Now

Upspeaking

Upspeaking is when declarative statements have a rising intonation at the end, making them sound more like a question.[25] Say, "Today is Thursday," and take note of what your voice does near the end of the statement. If the sound of your voice—your pitch—gets lower, then you are using downspeak. If your pitch gets higher, making it sound less like a statement and more like a question, you are using upspeak. Upspeak may make you seem less confident. Are you sure it's Thursday?

In her essay "Language in Society," UC Berkeley professor of linguistics Robin T. Lakoff explores how gender stereotypes condition women's speech. From her research, Lakoff identified that women often use what she refers to as "empty adjectives": adjectives that are vague and convey positivity, such as "gorgeous" or "adorable." Women also frequently use "tag questions," which require confirmation from someone else.[26] Asking "Tina is here, isn't she?"—when you know damn well that Tina would never miss an open bar and is probably already elbows deep in a Grey Goose martini while flirting shamelessly with the bartender who is young enough to be her son—is a tag question.

If your goal is to simply offer your ideas and knowledge like vegetables to a four-year-old, so they can be considered then flung onto the kitchen floor in favor of a simple carb covered in cheese, upspeaking, empty adjectives, and tag questions are exactly how you do it.

I Just Really Feel Like You Should Stop Apologizing (Does That Make Sense?)

Starting a sentence with "I feel like" is taking your argument, no matter how supported and well thought out, and turning it into a hunch.[27] You may be intending to create discussion or invite others to share their feelings, but what happens instead is that it ends the conversation. You can't argue with feelings.

"I just really feel like the return of *Sex and the City* fell flat without Kim Cattrall."

"No, it didn't. It's HBO's most-streamed series ever."

"Yeah, but I *felt* like it did."

How do you respond to that? That's right, you don't. The conversation is over. This may not present a problem when discussing unimportant things like a television show (not to say the *SATC* revival wasn't important; believe me, I know how important it was), but it becomes a major issue when discussing, say, why you should get a raise, why you're the best candidate for the job, or why a relationship needs to come to an end.

You don't "feel like" you deserve more money; you've been driving 70 percent of the company's revenue for the last eighteen months. You don't "just feel like" you can give little Quinn the seven-year-old, superhero-mermaid-cheerleader–themed sleepover birthday of her dreams; you have a portfolio of all the incredible parties you've planned and a mile-long list of glowing client testimonials. And you certainly don't "just really feel like" you need to end things with Steve. The man thinks the vulva is a car; it's time.

It's also time to stop apologizing, especially at work. Now, don't get it twisted: If you ate Alexa's clearly labeled lunch out of the communal fridge or backed into Modie's car in the parking lot, you owe her an apology, but it's time to stop apologizing when you haven't done anything wrong.

I see this all the time with my female college students. A young woman gets up to sing and before the first notes of the piano are even played, she apologizes for her voice which is "a little off" that day or that she is "just getting over a cold" or that "this might not be that good." Well, I don't know about you, but I can't wait to see her performance!

Her apology is a safety net in case things don't go as planned, which I totally get. Using your voice can be scary. Unfortunately, instead of catching her if she falls, that safety net is setting the expectation that she will. Imagine going to the new Meryl Streep movie and the opening credits say, "Starring Meryl Streep (sorry, this may not be her best work)." Ridiculous! Meryl works without a net, and so can you.

According to sociologist Dr. Maya Jovanovic in her popular TEDx talk on the subject, overapologizing occurs out of a desire to seem polite.[28] "Often times we think, 'Oh I'm being polite, they're going to perceive me as being a kind human being,'" Jovanovic said in a 2021 interview. "But in fact, we are perceived in the complete opposite way. In actuality, we are seen as not confident, as insecure, doubtful and incompetent."[29] Constant apologizing minimizes you and your accomplishments.[30] Trust me, the one thing you don't need to be is smaller.

Does that make sense? Yes, you make sense. Unless your audience has the brainpower of a Pet Rock or you are speaking Elvish, you are making sense. If you don't, someone will ask you to clarify.

How to Speak Like You Mean It

How you speak and the words you choose develop as a series of habits over time. Like most habits, you may not even be aware when you are doing them, and it's going to take some time to create change. Here's how to start.

Keep a Diary

You know food diaries, where you write down everything you ate that day and how much? This is like that, except it matters.

Over a few days, without working to change your behaviors, keep track of how many times you apologize, upspeak, or "just really feel like." You don't need to keep track of each of these; pick your poison. Before you can change your behavior, you need to become aware of it.

Once you get an idea of how often you're apologizing (or whichever habit you've chosen), take note of the circumstances around its use. Do certain people or situations trigger the apology? Do you most frequently apologize in emails? At meetings? When speaking to your boss? Your partner? Use this new information to make you more aware of how you're speaking when in these situations.

Sorry, Not Sorry

When the impulse to apologize strikes, evaluate whether an apology is truly warranted. If it is, then carry on, but if it's not, try using one of these alternatives:

> "*Unfortunately*, I won't have time for that today." You're busy, but you're not doing anything wrong.
>
> "*Excuse me*, I missed that, could you say it again?" The room is loud, but you're not doing anything wrong.
>
> "*Thank you for your patience*; it's been a crazy day." You're running a few minutes behind, but, again, you're not doing anything wrong.

Also, get in the habit of reading your emails and texts before you send them. A quick scan gives you the opportunity to change "Sorry, I didn't see this until right now" (which we all know is a lie) to a more truthful and unapologetic response: "If you email me after 8:00 p.m., know that I will be halfway through both a bottle of cab sauv and a rerun of *Master Chef Junior* and therefore will be unable to respond until tomorrow. Your patience is *so* appreciated."

The goal of the work in this chapter isn't to alter your authentic sound or to change your voice to meet some made-up societal standard. The goal is to help you sound confident, just as you are. Yes, these exercises are silly. They're weird. You might try them and think, "This is ridiculous; I sound terrible."

I'm going to tell you exactly what I tell my clients when they say those things to me (and they always say those things to me). First, I remind them that I'm really good at my job, and sending clients out into the world sounding like they spent a summer as a Guns N' Roses roadie would be really, really bad for business.

Then, I ask, "What's the worst that can happen? You look a little silly? You try something new and fail?" Guess what? If it's awful, we'll try it again. That's it. That's the worst thing that will happen—except maybe not trying at all and continuing to live silent and afraid, instead of speaking your mind, asking for what you want, and changing your entire life.

Summary

- The voice you hear in your head is never the same as the voice your audience hears. To truly hear what you sound like you *must* record yourself.
- Not only do women have to combat the stereotypes of what authority sounds like and what power and credibility look like, they also often have to speak using equipment that was created for men. Don't be afraid to advocate for yourself. When speaking at an event where you'll be using amplification, check in with the sound engineer and be sure to move the microphone so it's directly facing your mouth.
- You can speak louder; you have my permission. If you need to get louder without using a microphone, be sure to revisit my exercise on creating resonance. Resonance is using your air to get louder rather than then relying on your muscles alone.
- How you feel makes a *huge* difference in how you sound. It also makes a huge difference in how others respond to what you're saying. Use this knowledge to your advantage. Revisit my exercise on accessing emotion while speaking

and find the emotion that best fits your voice and your goals. Ask your friends for help.

- Be aware of pacing and pauses. Talk too quickly and your audience may miss vital information; too slowly, and even the most fascinating topic risks becoming snooze central. Keep your pace moderate and use pauses effectively. A great place to pause is wherever there would be punctuation; do not pause in the middle of a thought or word.
- It's okay to think these exercises are silly. They are. They're also incredibly effective. Think of the weight that will lift from your perfectly aligned shoulders when you no longer have to worry about sounding too shrill, too quiet, or too aggressive—because you *know* exactly how you sound. And if someone disagrees, send them my way.
- Upspeaking is when you raise your pitch at the end of a phrase, making it sound like a question rather than a statement. Upspeaking makes you seem less confident. So do empty adjectives (adjectives that are vague and generally positive, like "gorgeous" or "adorable") and tag questions (questions that ask someone else to confirm something you already know). Quit that shit now.
- Women are powerful, and their voices must reflect that power. Perhaps it isn't merely coincidence that society deems vocal fry, a popular vocal characteristic belonging to the most empowered generation of women ever, "annoying" and "unprofessional." Let's face it: It's easier to make fun of the sound of Jane's voice than to argue with her stance on critical race theory. Keep speaking authentically.

Chapter 5

Why Don't Women Speak Up?

It's Saturday morning and I'm giving a singing lesson in my home studio. It's my favorite room in the house: windows on two sides for lots of sunshine, direct access to the kitchen, and a door that locks. If you have kids, you get it. I'm just finishing up with Lizzie; she's fourteen and blessed with a cherub face, long strawberry-blond locks, and a naturally gifted singing voice. She's also one of the hardest-working singers I know, including the singers at the university where I'm on faculty and the professionals I have the pleasure of tuning up (pun intended) when needed.

We're nearing the end of the lesson, and I'm ready to ask her what I ask most of my students when we've spent significant time on a song: "On a scale of 1 to 10, with 1 being you're sitting on your couch in your pajamas singing along to a karaoke track and 10 being your debut performance at a sold-out Madison Square Garden, how did that go for you?" I'm excited to hear her answer because she's doing really, *really* good work: asking thoughtful questions and taking my adjustments like a pro.

Not to mention, this particular song is not the typical type she sings. It's crazy high and requires a lighter, more flexible sound that is not natural to her voice. She's Adele and this is totally Kate Bush or Joni Mitchell or Ani DiFranco. (If you need a musical reference from the last five years, I don't have one, so you're just going to have to trust me.) We're working on the song at Lizzie's request. She wanted to push herself. To explore a different sound. To expand. She didn't need to ask me twice.

"So, 1 to 10, how did that go for you?"

"Well . . ." She pauses, her body—moments ago alive with the energy of breath, sound, and story—stills and clenches. It's not a big change, but I notice. I notice because I've dedicated the last fifteen years of my life to noticing. I work with voices, and voices live and die in bodies, in minds, in breath. "I don't want to, you know, brag"—she looks down at the ground, at the rug I bought on sale at TJ Maxx three years ago that, trust me, is not worth looking at—"but I thought it was okay. It was pretty good."

Her words slap me in the face so hard I reflexively reach up and touch my cheek to soften the sting. I inhale sharply and close my eyes, searching for a response that is at once kind and the verbal equivalent of grabbing her by the shoulders and shaking vigorously. (I would follow through physically, but that might be bad for business.)

In my mind, I see Lizzie at age ten, showing up to my studio recital wearing high-top tennis shoes, knee-high socks, and a flower crown, along with the sundress her mama told me she was bribed into putting on. That moment is clearly sealed upon my heart both because she sang the absolute snot out of her song and also because she did it entirely and authentically as herself. Afterward, one of the parents in attendance, a working television and stage actor, commented, "That little girl needs her own TV show."

So what happened? Lizzie was still singing, still talking, still using the slang I pretend to understand then Google after she leaves, but she had lost her voice. In an article for the *Harvard Educational Review*, author and professor of psychoanalysis and clinical psychology Annie G. Rogers links the "ordinary courage" of adolescent girls with their ability to speak their truth. Rogers explains that around the year 1300, the word "courage"—originally from the Latin *cor*, meaning "heart," and *aetaticum*, meaning "age"—came to be closely associated with speaking. A popular definition of courage was "to speak one's mind by telling all one's heart."[1]

Sit. With. That. Lizzie's heart had been soaring the way a heart does when trial becomes triumph, when grit gives way to grace. I could literally see it. I was proud of her, and even more importantly, she was proud of herself. But instead of answering my question authentically, instead of speaking her mind by telling her heart, she lied. She hid behind her fear.

I wish I could say Lizzie's story is unique. I wish I could say that, sure, girls hit a rough patch in adolescence, but like my middle school crush on Nick Lachey and penchant for sparkly butterfly clips, they grow out of it; by sixteen they've found their voice again, and if not by sixteen, then definitely by twenty, or twenty-five, or thirty. I'd be lying. I have worked with singers, actors, teachers, business execs, and countless other women, young and young at heart, who depend on the use of their voice for their livelihoods, for their hobbies, and for their dreams. I have watched as they turn their trials into triumphs and then immediately refuse to take credit for their greatness. I have helped them prepare for an audition, a speech, a sales pitch, a job interview—for *months*—and then listened while they told me how they sat in the parking lot, too terrified to get out of the car.

It is time to get out of the car.

When I sat down to write this chapter, I started with a quick Google search: "Why don't women speak up?" Here's just a small sampling of my top results:

- Men Are Viewed as Leaders When They Speak Up, but Women Don't Get the Same Benefit[2]
- Why Women Are Less Likely to Speak Up in Public Than Men[3]
- Why It's So Hard to Speak Up against a Toxic Culture[4]

- The Truth about How Much Women Talk—and Whether Men Listen[5] (Spoiler alert: not enough on either count.)
- The Missing Women: Study finds that men speak twice as often as women do at colloquiums, a difference that can't be explained away by rank, speaker pool composition or women's interest in giving talks.[6]

I decided to read each of the articles, desperately hoping each link was clickbait, leading me to my free $1,000 Walmart gift card or a glimpse of celebrity porn rather than well-thought-out essays citing peer-reviewed studies from published journals. Two hours and a half-eaten box of cinnamon *Paw Patrol* snacks later, I closed my laptop, got the broom, and swept up my shattered hopes.

I don't know what I expected. As a vocal coach, I have seen and heard this scenario play out all too often. It usually goes something like this:

> *Client:* My high school choir director/ex-boyfriend/boss told me I don't have a very good voice/lack conviction/am too aggressive, so I just stopped singing/sharing/speaking up.
>
> *Me:* When did this happen?
>
> *Client:* Fifteen/twenty-six/last week. I just turned forty.

After I hand them a box of tissues and a shot of tequila (just kidding; I don't give them tissues), we stand up and start exploring their voice. By the end of the session, they're usually in a better place, and can—at least for the moment—believe they have the power to prove the naysayers wrong. Of course, as we'll explore in the coming chapters, creating lasting change to both your brain and your body takes time and practice. For now, let's take a look at when and how those habits start. (Spoiler alert: Puberty's a real bitch.)

What Happened to Miss Independent?

Ask an eight-year-old girl what she wants on her pizza and she'll tell you, "Pepperoni and cheese." Ask that same girl at fourteen and she says, "I don't care; what do you want?" Ask her at thirty-five and she doesn't answer because who fucking cares as long as she doesn't have to decide what's for dinner or cook it. (I'm a firm believer that once you can check the 35–41 box, you can and should say "fuck" more regularly.)

A director friend of mine always tells his actors to "play the positive." Even in dark scenes, find the humor, find the moments of light. It's hard to do, because as humans we naturally focus on the negative; we ruminate. (If you didn't know the word for replaying the last argument you had with your mother every day for a week, now you do.) Women partake in this particular pastime more than men do, often getting hooked on the negative during puberty. I totally get this. The moment in art class when the love of my sixth grade life announced that I had "way more" of a mustache than he did comes immediately to mind, but among the zits, hips, and curly hair that had yet to find its diffuser, I'm sure there are others.

Middle school also marks the start of rewarding "good-girl behavior": Sit quietly. Follow the rules. Get good grades. Earn gold stars.[7] In middle school, the kids who don't cause problems are rewarded. Which, as someone who has had the absolute pleasure of teaching many an after-school drama program to middle schoolers, I also totally get. After two hours standing powerless on a cafetorium stage while a pack of feral twelve-year-olds runs in circles around the room, screaming at the top of their lungs, you too would give the leading role to Sara Sims, who is sitting quietly in the first row—integrity of *Toy Story Jr.* be damned.

The problem with rewarding good-girl behavior is that it ingrains in young women the idea that to be quiet is to be good, which can only mean that being loud is bad. To listen is to be good, to follow is to be good, to accept is to be good; to speak up, to lead, to question, to challenge is to be in trouble. This behavior might earn middle school gold stars, but when the classroom turns into the boardroom, the rules change. As adults, we look for leaders who are challengers, risk-takers who have novel ideas and out-of-the-box ways of thinking. Girls who were rewarded for not speaking up become women who don't know how to.

This phenomenon is clearly seen in male-dominated fields like STEM. Alexandra Knight is the founder of STEMAZING, a UK-based community of trailblazing women who are committed to breaking down stereotypes in STEM and forging a more "STEMAZING" future for the next generation. I've had the pleasure of speaking with Alex on several occasions and am blown away by her knowledge, passion, and commitment not only to empowering women but also to turning them into role models for young girls. When I was working on this chapter, I knew I needed her input and asked her to share what inspired her to start STEMAZING and what keeps her passion burning:

> There is a lack of women in STEM, and particularly engineering, because of gender stereotypes. The historical great engineers like [Isambard Kingdom] Brunel; he had a sister, Sophia, who apparently had just as much potential as an engineer but never became one because women were not allowed to access those opportunities. We are trying to break into industries that have historically been designed for men, by men. Even now, all the solutions we're designing in the STEM industry, we're risking those being designed for men, by men, especially white men, so it's critical that we change gender stereotypes at very young ages, three to five years old and up.
>
> We need a lot more investment in getting diverse role models into media, into schools, into our books, and into the ways society perceives stereotypes in STEM. The global challenges we're facing in the next couple of years absolutely need diverse teams in stem to solve them.[8]

As the mother of two young daughters, Alex's words struck a chord with me. I tell my daughters they can grow up to be anything they want to. My five-year old's current career choice is mermaid, but in case that doesn't work out, I want her to have role models. I want her to see strong women leading in fields from STEM to the arts to business and everywhere in between.

Why Women Don't Speak Up at Work

Back in the early 2000s I was working for a theatre company that created ESL-focused children's productions in South Korea. (Yes, that's a real job.) I was freshly out of college and a seventeen-year career as a rule-following, straight-A-getting good girl. I was also (1) in a country I couldn't find on a map and (2) alone. So I did what I did best: kept my head down, did good work, and listened to my boss without question. One night over drinks, my boss told me that when his contract was up, he would love to see me take over his role. I just needed to speak up more.

Around the six-month mark, I started to find my footing in the country and in the company. I took on more responsibility, made friends, and regularly spent half my paycheck on AAA-quality fake designer handbags bought from an elderly Korean couple who sold them out of their apartment in black trash bags while communicating only via walkie-talkie. I also took my boss's advice and started asking more questions. I had ideas, suggestions, and critiques, so I shared them, even if they were of my superiors. It felt good. It felt . . . adult.

Then, suddenly, my boss announced he wasn't renewing his contract and in-house interviews for his position would be starting the following week. I was stoked. It was my first chance at leadership, and I knew he wanted to give me the job. It was in the bag, and that bag had a silver *C* for Chanel on it.

My interview went a little something like this:

Me: Thank you for meeting with me. Here are sixteen ideas on how we can improve our quality of company life, work, and creative output *and* put more butts in seats at our shows.

My boss: You know, Jessica. You've really changed. You used to just be so . . . easy. Just ask Jessica and she's on it. Now, I don't know; honestly, you can be difficult.

Me: I'm sorry, am I not subservient enough for you anymore? Is the quality of my ideas diminished by the volume and frequency of my speaking them? Are you threatened that a twenty-three-year-old woman with a fierce pixie cut and an almost real magenta Birkin bag has plans to fix what you could not? Or do I just make your dick feel small?

At least that's what I said in my head, to my shower wall, and in the bathroom mirror for the next six weeks. In the moment, I'm pretty sure I mumbled something like, "Thank you for your time" before drowning myself in a bottle of soju. Sound familiar? (Want to drown the fear without the hangover? Check out chapter 7.)

In *Speaking While Female*, Sheryl Sandberg calls this phenomenon "the tightrope."[9] At work, women are either barely heard or they're too aggressive. Follow the "good-girl" rules, and you're told to speak up. Speak up, and you're difficult. Being a woman isn't walking a tightrope; it's walking a tightrope backward, in heels.

More importantly, why do we care so damn much? I was in a meeting when a male member of my team shared an opinion that was totally and completely incorrect. It contradicted scientific research, and more importantly, it contradicted what I teach and was causing confusion among our students. To be clear, I was the senior faculty member in this situation. I was the expert. So I corrected him. I politely but firmly told him to stay in his lane.

When the meeting ended, I had hives from my collarbone to my chin. I immediately sent a text to my friend, who was also in the meeting, asking him if I came down too hard with my critique.

"I didn't mean to upset anyone. Was what I said okay?" What the hell? Why was I reacting this way?

I am an actress. I have sung by myself in front of *thousands* of people, by choice. I have missed holidays, birthdays, and my little brother's college graduation to be on stage, speaking and singing in front of people who paid a lot of money to be there watching me. I teach actors and singers at the university level in the same program that trained Sandra Bullock. (Obviously, I wasn't there as I am *several* years younger than Sandy, but you see my point.)

I—an actress and professor with advanced degrees and more than fifteen years of experience who teaches an eight-week course on *overcoming performance anxiety*—sat there flustered and flushed after a thirty-minute meeting where I had to tell a twenty-five-year-old fetus to stay in his lane. Why did I care so damn much?

I cared because I wanted to be liked more than I wanted to be respected. This need was so strong, so ingrained, that I didn't even recognize it existed. But there it was. In fact, upon further examination, this particular brand of crazy showed up on the reg in the form of my good friend passive aggression. In the words of Addison Montgomery-Shepherd, "There is a land called Passive Aggressiva, and I am their queen."[10]

While I was too scared to rock the boat face-to-face, I was a master of smiling sweetly while simultaneously eviscerating my opponent in my mind—that, or a vigorous, head-nodding assurance that everything was "just fine" followed by the double finger and a silent "Fuuuuuck Youuuuu" once I'd retreated to the safety of my locked office door.

Sound familiar? I thought so. Recently, one of my best girlfriends and I were discussing her new boss:

"She's just so full of herself."

"Agreed."

"I'm so uncomfortable being around her. She's so rude. Last week, when I posted a picture of our new trampoline, she called my daughter a spoiled brat on Facebook. First of all, she's not a brat. She's a very kind, empathetic little girl. Second of all, the trampoline was a reward for something we've worked on for *months* with lots of tantrums and tears. And you know what, even if it wasn't, it's none of her business what I buy my daughter. If I want to buy her a pony because it's Tuesday, I can and it's none of her goddamn business!"

"So true."

"Plus, I spent, like, a month writing that report, and she couldn't find half an hour to read it? Really? Does she not value my work at all?"

"Did you ask her that?"

"No, I'm extra nice to her. She has no idea what's going on in my mind. Sometimes I even feel bad for being so shitty to her in my head. Okay, I've got to go, I'm meeting her for lunch."

To be clear, this is not healthy behavior. Now, I am not advocating cussing out your boss or very publicly telling the bitchy mom at playgroup exactly where she can stick her dairy-free, gluten-free, nut-free snacks, but not voicing your true feelings isn't helping anyone. Not the object of your aggression, who has no idea that their behavior is causing you distress, and therefore, has no opportunity to change it. And certainly not you, who now spends the evenings reliving a stressful situation over and over, stuck in an emotional shithole of your own making, while Becky and Rhonda go for post-work tapas and tequila, blissfully unaware that anything is wrong.

Why Women Don't Speak Up in Relationships

Before I met my husband, I spent two years in a relationship where the more serious things got, the more time I spent in the shower chanting, "You don't have to marry him, you don't have to marry him, you don't have to marry him," like a desert monk, while Celine Dion's "I've Got Nothing Left," ran on a loop in the background. Really. During those two years, my one-and-only told me I was "difficult," "wishy-washy," "too sensitive," and "tough to be with." And I believed him. (Side note: If you're already nodding your head because you've been there, ask yourself, in your whole life has anyone else *ever* repeatedly said such things about you? Then, baby, *maybe it's not you.*)

This story gets worse before it gets better. When my better half told me I was the "biggest girl" he'd ever been with, I stopped eating everything that wasn't kale and ran myself ragged at the gym while convincing myself he "just wants me to be healthy." I even had a consultation to get totally non-FDA-approved weight loss injections a dancer friend of mine told me about, which *might* cause my hair to fall out and would *definitely* mean the end of my libido but *could* help spot-reduce my "problem areas." I know what you're thinking: "I can tell you how to spot reduce a 'problem area'—break up with it." But to do that, I needed to face the fear of being alone and her ride-or-dies: the fear of rejection and the fear of failure. And they are some mean girls.

About six months in, on the cusp of our relationship becoming something more serious, my bae told me he couldn't see a future for us in the long term because he could never be with someone who believed in God. And instead of saying, "Okay, well, thank you for your time" and running back to my apartment as fast as my Uggs could carry me, I turned my back on my faith. I questioned something I have known in my heart to be true for as long as I can remember.

I was raised Catholic: a Mass-every-Sunday, no-meat-on-Friday, my-favorite-aunt-is-a-nun kind of Catholic. My friends and I traded sins before confession the way other kids traded Pokémon cards:

"I'm going in with talking back to my mom."

"Didn't you use that last week?"

"Can I use it again?"

"No, he'll think you didn't really repent."

"*Shit!* Oh! Yes! I'm going in with swearing."

Over the years, my belief system has strayed from the path of Catholicism. I love the tradition of it: the hymns, the smell of incense, the offering of peace, the fact that anywhere you go Mass will always be an hour (forty-five minutes if you leave after Communion). But I simply cannot worship at the same altar where women aren't allowed to lead, where my LGBTQIA+ friends are seen as less than, and where we proclaim that we are the one true church, following the one true God, on the one and only path to salvation. We are right, and the other five and a half billion people on the planet are headed for the fiery pits of doom. However, I never have, and never will, stop trusting that I am part of something greater than myself and that that something is pure love.

I felt ashamed of this part of my story for a long time. I no longer do—forgiveness is truly the greatest gift—but it's a part of my story that I still, more than a decade later, don't readily share. Because who *does* that? What kind of woman trades in her faith for a guy who tells her she is an overly emotional fatty who lacks conviction and is really tough to love? What kind of woman is so desperate to be loved, so desperate to be accepted, so desperate to prove that she is worthy of being someone's someone that she would literally question the one constant in her life?

A normal one. I'm going to tell you what a very wise therapist told me: If you haven't struggled in a relationship with someone else, with yourself, with a substance, with a habit, with getting out of bed in the morning—you are not exceptional, you are lucky. Life is messy. Growing is hard. It's hard at fourteen, and it is still really fucking hard at almost forty. I share my story not because it's exceptional, but because if there's even the slightest chance you see yourself in it, I want you to know that change is possible. You already have all the tools to face your fears and change your life; they are within you, right now. You are enough. You are enough. You are so enough, you don't even know how enough you are.

It should also warm your heart to know that my ex now lives in a commune in rural Colorado raising homing pigeons and working as both an astrologer and pet psychic. I'll put his website in the appendix in case you or your goldendoodle want to get in touch.

Shift the Shit

Your brain is incredible: virtually limitless information storage, processing speeds upward of 260 mph, more than a hundred thousand neurons in a tissue sample the size of a single grain of sand. Your brain hosts the world's most powerful tech. It's even better than the iPhone 14.

Your thoughts have power. In fact, your thoughts are so powerful that your brain treats *thinking* and *doing* the same way. Just thinking about an action causes the same motor neurons to fire as actually doing the action.[11] I thought my way through a fierce core workout last night while drinking a glass of Shiraz. Amazing.

The thinking/doing also applies to your fight-or-flight response: that shaky-legs, dry-mouth, sweaty-palms, forgot-your-own-name routine I talked about in chapter 2. The more negative self-talk you do, the stronger the response becomes, until you find yourself in the Target parking lot, white-knuckling the steering wheel of your parked SUV and sweating through your shirt because you thought about the presentation you're giving at work . . . next month.

What's a girl to do? It's time to shift the shit. Your brain *loves* repetition, and she also *loves* relationships, attaching new information to old. So it's time to change the way you think about speaking up. Here's how:

1. Write down a sentence highlighting your strongest fears about speaking in public. For example: "I hate speaking in public. I always forget what I want to say and look totally unprepared.
2. Shift the shit. Flip that sentence inside out: "I love public speaking. I always speak clearly and effectively and look totally prepared."
3. Write your new sentence down three times. Post-it notes are great, but if you want to go total Lisa Frank with this, I won't stop you.
4. Post your sentences in places you see often. Your bedside table is required (sleep is *key* to creating lasting memories); I also recommend your bathroom mirror, your desk, and your steering wheel.
5. Read your sentence aloud: before bed and when you wake up, for sure—and any other time you see it.
6. When negative thoughts arise, shut them down before they get one Jimmy Choo in the door. Instead, repeat your new, positive sentence.
7. Rinse and repeat. Watch your thought patterns begin to shift. You are amazing.

Summary

- The fear of speaking up often begins in middle school, when girls are rewarded for sitting quietly and following directions. This "good-girl behavior" works really well until adulthood, when the script flips and leaders are seen as out-of-the-box thinkers who question convention. Girls who are rewarded for not speaking up become women who don't know how to.

- It is more important to be respected than it is to be liked. I'm going to repeat that. It is more important to be *respected* than it is to be *liked*. I didn't like my midwife when she yelled, "Jessica, there's no time for an epidural, the only way the pain is going to end is to have this baby," but you better believe I respect the hell out of her for not taking any of my shit and delivering my daughter safely.
- Speaking up can have consequences. Things don't always go the way you planned. I'm going to go out on a limb and say that if asking questions and offering differing opinions loses you a promotion or gets you fired, you didn't want that job anyway.
- Not telling people they've wronged you doesn't help anyone: not the object of your aggression, who has no idea something is amiss and therefore can't change the offending behavior, and not you, who is now wasting your valuable time ruminating on the event rather than eating delicious food or having great sex or building your empire.
- If you haven't struggled in a relationship with someone else, with yourself, with a substance, with a habit, with getting out of bed in the morning—you are not exceptional, you are lucky. Life is messy. We're all doing the best we can. Speak truth. Give grace.

Chapter 6

Impost-Her Syndrome

At my workshops, I always start by telling the group of women I'm working with who I am and what I'm all about. I hope I've made both of those things clear by now, but in case you missed it:

> Hi, I'm Jessica and I'm a professor, researcher, and vocal coach who is hell-bent on helping women harness the power of their voices. I'm here today because I'm really tired of watching women live in silent mediocrity and fear, when they have the power to use their voices to get the hell up and out. I'm passionate about my family, my friends, and my work, and I strongly believe any candy that isn't chocolate is inferior.

Nice to make your acquaintance.

After that, I ask anyone else who'd like to share who they are and why they decided to come. At my last workshop, a woman raised her hand and shared her story, and it stuck to me so hard I need to share it here. It went something like this:

> Hi everyone, I'm Rachel. I'm an attorney. Well, actually I have my JD/MD, so I guess I'm technically a doctor too. I recently made partner at my firm, and I'm terrified someone is going to

walk into my office and say, "Who let you in here? You don't belong here. Get out."

Let's just unpack this for a moment. Rachel—who, by the way, was gorgeous and didn't look a day over thirty—wasn't content with just being a doctor or a lawyer, so *she became both*. She overachieved the overachievers. She passed the boards and the bar. She made partner, which is like, *really* hard to do, and did it before she was forty. And she was terrified that someone was going to call her bluff. Um, what?

Rachel was suffering from something I like to call "Impost-Her Syndrome." Impost-Her Syndrome is when women—educated, qualified, experienced women—still think they aren't good enough. Now, I am not a therapist, so I'm not even going to attempt to analyze the events that led Rachel to this particular point in her journey, but what I am going to do is tell her, and you, that this is not okay. It is not okay for anyone, even the voice in your head, to deny your worth.

You know what voice I'm talking about, right? The one that shows up when you have an idea for a new business, think about finishing your college degree, or decide to say no instead of people-pleasing. I have that voice. As I mentioned earlier, her name is Sheila, and she can get real mouthy.

I highly recommend you name your voice too. That way, when someone hears you talking to yourself in the Target dressing room you can pretend you're actually on the phone with your bitchy older sister: "Shut the hell up, Kathy; chartreuse is for everyone!"

Hold Yourself Accountable

I also recommend you start a Bullshit Journal. Buy a little notebook or start a folder on your phone where you can call yourself out on your bullshit in real time. Mine is baby pink with gold hearts on the front. The purchase was inspired by my favorite store during my time in Seoul, called Fucking Lovely, which sold women's fashions and little girls' clothes that were all—you guessed it!—fucking lovely. Keep your Bullshit Journal close by; that way, when Sheila starts acting up, instead of trying to ignore her—which, let's be honest, never works—you can record the thought in real time and pay closer attention to it.

For example, if you're considering going for a big promotion at work and start thinking, "I'm never going to get this. I'm not qualified, and even if by some miracle they do think I'm qualified, I can't lead a team. Who's going to listen to me?" stop and write it down. Then give a little thought to what triggered your reaction in the first place. Is it that you're younger than the people you'll be leading? Been at the company for a shorter amount of time? Afraid of leading weekly team meetings and commanding the room? (Side note: If it's the last one, you totally bought the right book.)

When you look at the underlying fears, I'm hoping you'll get a sense of what you can control versus what you can't. Letting go of what you can't control is a *huge* part of my work with young actors. Each spring, we announce what the next year's plays and musicals will be, and from that moment until auditions during the first week of classes the following fall, the name of the student game is panic. The students try to figure out what songs they should sing and what monologues they should present to give them the best chance of being cast in the role of their hearts' desire. For most of them, this means trying to figure out not what materials best show off their skills, but what they think the director wants to see.

In the words of my dear friend and brilliant director Bryan Conger, who faces this wave of panic head on, "Stop. Stop trying to figure out what I want and start showing me what you do best." Why? First, sometimes I don't know for sure what I want until I see it. Second, I might really have an idea of what I want, but I'd love for someone to change my mind. Third—and this is the most important one—it is a waste of time to spend months worrying about something you have no control over. Do you think Bryan is spending his summer worrying about who he's going to cast in the fall musical? No. He's drinking sweet tea and floating on a pool noodle in Pamlico Sound off the side of my boat while my five-year-old daughter asks him for the hundredth time to watch her poorly executed handstand.

Prepare? Yes. Prepare like crazy for your interview, pitch, speech, or presentation. Preparation is so important I wrote a whole chapter about it in this book. There is no better feeling than leaving the room feeling like you did exactly what you went in there to do. But then you have to *let it go*. You can spend hours intricately analyzing every question, laugh, head nod, and brow furrow in the room, and guess what? You will be no closer to your goal.

In addition to writing down the negative thought and what triggered it, I like to take note of whether the fear is in my control. *I'm younger than the team I'd be leading*. Nope, not in my control. *The investor will like my product but have a similar one in her portfolio*. Not in my control. *I won't have answers to their questions, or I will but won't be able to communicate them clearly*. In my control and something I can prepare for.

Put Your Negativity on Trial

You can also challenge yourself to turn the negative statements into questions:

1. Think about your most common Impost-Her fears and worries, then write down your answers to these prompts in your journal.
    a. OMG I am so . . .
    b. I can't . . .
    c. I'll never . . .
2. Challenge yourself. Turn each statement into a question.

a. OMG I am so . . . ?

b. I can't . . . ?

c. I'll never . . . ?

Are you sure? Are you *absolutely positive* that the answer to each question is yes? Says who? And when? Now, think about all the times you weren't. All the times you did. Ask yourself instead, "What if I could?"

Here's an example:

1. Let's say your current Impost-Her syndrome centers around the job you want but keep telling yourself you'll never get. Here we go:

    a. OMG I am so bad at interviewing.

    b. I can't answer questions on the spot.

    c. I'll never get my dream job.

2. Challenge yourself. Turn each statement into a question.

    a. OMG I am so bad at interviewing?

    b. I can't answer questions on the spot?

    c. I'll never get my dream job?

Are you so bad at interviewing? Are you absolutely sure the answer is yes? Let's look at the opposing evidence. You are currently employed in a job you had to interview for. So you've had at least one successful interview, if not more, depending on the hiring process. You've been employed at one job or another since you were eighteen and started waiting tables at Applebee's. Each of these positions involved at least one interview, which must have ended successfully, since you were hired. Let's say you're thirty-eight. That's *twenty years* of being hired by companies after your interview. You might not like interviewing, you might be scared of interviewing, but are you *so* bad at interviewing? Sorry, but the evidence points to no.

Next: You can't answer questions on the spot? Are you a Miranda or a Charlotte? I'm a Carrie. Superman or Batman? Obviously Superman, unless you're talking Christian Bale's Batman, in which case, it's a coin flip. Chocolate or strawberry? Chocolate. Cabernet or Chardonnay? Yes. See, you can totally answer questions on the spot! In all seriousness, though, the evidence from the previous question points to you being able to answer questions on the spot. Are your answers always perfect? Probably not. Could you improve your ability to gather your thoughts quickly and state them clearly when under pressure? Probably. But are you incapable of answering questions on the spot? It's a no for me.

Your dream job: Are you sure you'll never get it? Really? Have you applied? If the answer to that question is no, then you're right, you'll never get your dream job. The same applies if your dream job is to own a business, write books, or teach cooking lessons. Have you tried? In the words of my husband's ninety-four-year-old grandmother in her commercial for Gun Lake Casino: "You can't win, if you don't play."

Are you underqualified? Okay, then get qualified. Turned down? Okay, then get a coach, take some classes, or ask for feedback. Successful people make it look easy, but that does not mean it *is* easy.

THE *AMERICAN IDOL* EFFECT

When *American Idol* came out, everyone thought they were a singer. It did not matter if you had taken singing lessons, sung in a choir, or practiced singing a single day in your life. People lined up around the block to tell the world how they were destined for stardom because their great-aunt Nancy thinks their rendition of "Jolene" sounds just like a young Dolly Parton. Because great singing looks effortless.

Every year I ask my freshmen, wouldn't it be nice if you could sing from the bottom of your range to the top of your range, make no adjustments, and have everything move smoothly and all the notes be full and clear? I ask this question about halfway through fall semester, once they've gotten a taste of the *constant* adjustments that need to be made to achieve this but haven't yet mastered the new skills. At this point, the chances of any given voice lesson erupting into tears is about 70/30.

This question always gets a laugh, not because it's funny but because it's absurd. Yes, of course it would be nice to just show up and be able to do this incredibly nuanced, difficult thing perfectly. But unless your name is Jennifer Hudson, it's not going to happen. Actually, even if your name *is* Jennifer Hudson, it's not going to happen. I say this not because Jennifer's God-given talent isn't out-of-this-world amazing but because saying that she can "just do it" implies that she doesn't work her ass off on the regular keeping her voice in shape and perfecting her craft.

The same can be said about being successful at just about anything. My father is one of the leading authors and speakers in the country on how the brain learns. We were presenting at a national education conference together a few years ago and sitting in on a session where the presenter talked about Structured Learning Assistance (SLA) being the new hot thing used and referenced nationwide. My dad leaned over to me and whispered, "Judy Hooper and I invented SLA in the '90s." Mic drop.

My dad refers to himself as a "twenty-year overnight success"—meaning he's been doing the work for twenty years and only recently did the greater public start to pay attention. This is the other reality of success: It takes time. This can be a difficult concept in a culture that worships at the altar of now. Going for your dreams often takes patience and it takes resilience.

LEARN TO FAIL SPECTACULARLY

In October 2021, I was interviewed by *Thrive Global* for the series "Rising through Resilience."[1] The pandemic had been in full swing for more than a year and the magazine was featuring stories of courage during turbulent times. The interviewer led with the question, "How would you define resilience?"

After I Googled resilience, just to double-check I had the definition right (true story), I started talking about how, for me, resilience begins with the voice. It's choosing to speak up for yourself and your dreams, even in the face of adversity. See, adversity often begets silence, and silence often equals acceptance. Maybe you don't know the first step to take toward your dream, so you stay still. Maybe there are too many unknowns or too many risks between here and there, so you don't try. Maybe you think your voice doesn't matter, your dreams are too big, or past failures mean you are forever destined to fail. Resilience is choosing to try and try again. It's the rebound.

Failure isn't an end; it's the ultimate new beginning. I treasure failure. You make a choice and it doesn't work out. Great! Put it on the list of what not to do, and try again. I see resilient people as being creative and courageous. To be resilient is to realize there must be more than one way to get where you want to go. To be courageous, you have to keep going until you find it.

WHERE DOES IMPOST-HER SYNDROME COME FROM?

You've named your inner voice and started keeping track of your fears and self-critique in your journal, so you're getting an idea of what triggers them and whether or not they hold up under cross-examination. But why do you have these doubts at all? Where does Impost-Her Syndrome come from?

According to Ruchika Tulshyan and Jodi Ann Burey in an article in the *Harvard Business Review*, "Women don't belong, because we were never supposed to belong."[2] Let's look at the evidence. Women got the right to vote on August 18, 1920.[3] Not great, but that was more than a hundred years ago. What about taking out a credit card in her own name? 1974. Not being fired for being pregnant? 1978. Not having to have sex with her husband even though he wanted to? 1993. Serving her country in combat? 2013.[4] Making the same amount of money as a man for doing the same job? Being completely in charge of her own body? Being equally represented in the news media, the C-suite, and on stage and screen? I'll keep you posted.[5]

When Kamala Harris was elected, I sat my five-year-old daughter down and tried to explain to her what it meant that this woman—this beautiful brown woman—was now the vice president of our country. Then I closed my eyes and fervently prayed that my daughter never has to have this conversation with her daughter, that she never has to explain what a big deal it is for a woman to lead our country because, in her world, women always have.

No Girls Allowed

It's not shocking that women feel like they don't belong to a club that requires its members to be straight, white, male . . . and not much else. It is shocking that according to the data, *a lot* of women are feeling this way. The tax, audit, and advisory firm KPMG polled 750 high-performance, executive women who were at, or very near, the C-suite and had taken part in the firm's Women's Leadership Summit. Of those women, 75 percent said they had experienced imposter syndrome at some point during their career and 81 percent believed they put more pressure on themselves to succeed than their male counterparts did.[6]

As part of my assistantship in grad school, I had to participate in the university's annual opera production. My first year, the opera featured an entirely female cast and was being directed not by the head of the voice department, who usually took the helm, but by a female professor. I was really excited to work with her. She was close to my age, we had mutual friends in the business, and she had completed her doctorate at one of the most competitive voice programs in the nation. She was (and still is) a total rock star.

On our first day of rehearsal, everyone in the cast arrived early. The rehearsal room was quite literally humming with the energy and voices of thirty young female artists on the verge of diving into a new piece of work. When our director entered, accompanied by the head of the voice department, we stood in unison and applauded. She stood in front of us wearing three-inch heels, a killer wrap dress, and a no-nonsense expression. She looked feminine, strong, and a little bit scary. I wanted to be her when I grew up.

Once we quieted down, the very male, very straight, very white head of the voice department stood in front of this room of young women and introduced the director of our production as "Miss." Not "Doctor," not even "Professor," but "Miss." I watched her as he said it and saw how her gaze narrowed, her lips pursed, and her fingers pressed into the sides of the binder she was holding.

I immediately raised my hand with a question I already knew the answer to, simply so I could direct it to her and refer to her, very emphatically, as "Doctor." I wanted her to know that I saw her. I felt for her. Here we were, a room full of women, and it took the one and only man less than a sentence to downgrade our leader.

Was his statement malicious? Probably not, though I'm not sure if that makes it better or worse: better, because it means he's not a complete asshole, and I like to think everyone is basically good inside; worse, because it means his response was conditioned.

It's the riddle about the boy who, while driving to school with his dad, gets in a car accident and is taken to the hospital. When he arrives in the emergency room, the doctor sees him and says, "Oh my God, that's my son." How is this possible? To which the answer, obviously, is: Why is this a riddle at all?

What Can You Do?

What can you do when you find yourself doubting your greatness? When you catch yourself chalking your accomplishments up to "dumb luck" or "just timing"? When the weight of being the first, the only, or one of the few threatens to pull you under? Here are a few suggestions.

Make a List of What You're Good At

When I was a senior in college, a professor sat my class down in a circle and asked us, "What are you good at?" I was confused. I'd spent the last four years being told what I needed to work on, where I needed to improve, and then having that improvement critiqued, but this was the first time anyone had asked me what I was good at. Honestly, I was twenty-two years old, and it was the first time in my entire life anyone had asked that question.

Looking around the circle at my classmates' furrowed brows and fidgety fingers, I got the impression it was their first time too. No one answered. No one even looked up. We sat in complete silence for what felt like an eternity until finally a girl raised her hand and said meekly, "I guess I'm good at singing high notes. I mean, they sound okay." Her eyes darted nervously around the circle, as if she was waiting for someone to yell, "You're lying! Your high notes suck!"

Thankfully, that didn't happen—and you know what? In the fifteen years I've been teaching, I've asked hundreds of students this same question, and that's never happened. Not once. What does happen, and what happened that day in my class, is that one by one the students speak up. With each person who shares, the room gets a little bit warmer. The eyes start to look somewhere other than the floor. The shoulders lower. There's a collective exhale. You're really damn good at something, and it's time to let everyone—especially yourself—know it.

Start by making a list. Think of your own Impost-Her Syndrome. It can be personal or professional. Now write down five things you're *really* good at or ways you *really* show up in this area. Start with five, but if the ideas start flowing, go with it. I'm not going to stop your greatness.

Maybe you doubt yourself in a new position of leadership. Start by thinking back to why you wanted the position in the first place. I'm guessing it was because you saw problems and had solutions. You had a vision of how great your company or organization could be and a clear plan to get there. You're organized. You have killer time management skills. Your superpower is inspiring others to be their best selves.

Maybe you really want to start your own business but doubt your ability to be successful. Why do you want to start it? Why do you lay awake at night mentally designing menus, scanning office space rentals, or writing curriculum? Because you *know* in your gut that the world needs your red wine–braised short ribs. You *know* you should have your own practice and stop being overworked and underpaid. You *know* young brains weren't designed to learn sitting quietly at desks for hours on end. There's a problem, and the solution is you.

Remember: It's Not Just Luck

When it comes to success, women often describe themselves as lucky rather than skilled.[7]

> "I'm so lucky to have gotten where I am."
>
> "I'm so lucky to be surrounded by such a great team."
>
> "I'm so lucky my husband figured out where my clitoris is."

Why do women attribute their success to luck rather than education, experience, and tenacity? We've been conditioned to. Sheryl Sandberg, arguably one of the most successful women on the planet, who literally created a movement of female empowerment with *Lean In*, was described by the *New York Times* as "lucky."[8] The exact quote, "She's wickedly smart, but she's lucky," was in reference to critique of Sandberg's TED Talk, which attributed success to a woman's ambition and confidence but neglected to mention the barriers many women face due to decades of sexism in the workplace.

The problem with the quote, according to Rebecca J. Rosen, writing in a piece for the *Atlantic* titled "In the New York Times, Sheryl Sandberg Is Lucky, Men Are Good," isn't the critique, it's the use of the word "but."[9] "But" implies that Sandberg is smart, but her business savvy is trumped by her luck. Let's be clear: Sheryl Sandberg is privileged, and she knows it. She begins her now famous TED Talk by saying, "Let's start out by admitting we're lucky." Her message to her audience of highly educated, privileged women is not to deny your privilege but to stop crediting it entirely for your success.

A few months ago, I started working with an LA-based client who is a talented singer/songwriter. She had been playing open mics and had a few gigs at clubs, and her music was starting to gain a following. During one of our sessions, she mentioned to me that a family friend of hers is a music exec at a major record label. He'd offered to listen to her songs and give her feedback, but so far, she hadn't taken him up on it.

Here is this gorgeous, talented young woman hustling from open mic to open mic, trying to get her songs heard by the right people, and when exactly *the* right person offers to listen to her music—she says no. I'm sorry, what?!? After I closed my gaping mouth, I gently asked her why she hadn't used him as a resource. Her answer? She felt like having access to him was cheating.

Do you know what Norah Jones, Miley Cyrus, and Nancy Sinatra have in common? Norah Jones may have been born into the music industry, but I'm willing to bet the six billion people who have streamed her songs didn't do it because her dad is a world-famous sitar player. The thing about having access is that while it may open a door, it's still up to you to get yourself through it.

If you're reading this book from a place of privilege and access, give thanks for it, and then refuse to let it go to waste. Recognize that yes, you are lucky—*and* you are ambitious, tenacious, and highly skilled. Work your network and work it unapologetically. It does not matter who opens the door; what matters is that you're ready to step through it.

Expect Imperfection

You are going to fail. You are going to fail hard. A lot. You're going to make the wrong choice, take the wrong road, be with the wrong partner, and give the wrong answer. The sooner you accept that you are not now and will never, ever be perfect, the sooner you can stop chasing perfection and start living in all your messy, human glory.

When a woman fails, she is likely to doubt her own abilities or knowledge; when a man fails, he's more likely to blame outside factors: the temperature of the room, a faulty microphone, or an inattentive audience. Rather than seeing failure objectively, women often take it personally, believing *they* are inherently flawed.[10] Then they stop taking risks.

When you find yourself hesitant to take a risk, fearing failure or still reeling from a recent fail, try asking yourself these questions based on work by Dr. Kristin Neff, professor of educational psychology at the University of Texas at Austin and an expert in the field of self-compassion:

1. What advice would you give your best friend? If someone you care about was scared to take a risk because she might fail, or fail again, what would you say to her? What about post-failure? What if your best girlfriend didn't get the job or bombed the speech? How would you pick her back up? Now, try talking to yourself the same way. You are someone you care about too.

2. How do you really feel? Stop spiraling. Don't inflate what really happened, but don't deny it either. You panicked during an interview. Be clear: You're embarrassed and disappointed. You're not worthless. You're not a failure. You're not doomed to walk the earth unemployed and alone until you finally just give up, lay down in a ditch on the side of the road, and succumb to scurvy.

3. What's the worst that can happen? Do you have the skills and support system to deal with that outcome? And finally, to quote my mother's personal slogan, and the obvious title should a documentary ever be made about my childhood: What have you learned from this? (The Jessica Doyle-Mekkes story).

4. Are you truly alone? Remind yourself that failure happens to everyone. Katy Perry was dropped from three record labels before finding success with Capitol Music Group. *Harry Potter* was rejected by all twelve major publishers in the UK before Bloomsbury took a chance on the then-unknown J. K. Rowling. Even Oprah Winfrey was fired from her first television job.[11] There is not a person on earth who hasn't dropped a few balls. The great thing about balls? They bounce.[12]

Summary

- Impost-Her Syndrome is when women—educated, qualified, experienced women—think they aren't good enough. It's the voice that shows up when you have an idea for a new business, think about finishing your college degree, or decide to say no instead of people-pleasing. The one that whispers, "You can't do that. It's too hard. Think about what people will say."

- Start a journal where you can call yourself out on your bullshit in real time. Then think about what triggered your reaction in the first place. Get a sense of what you can control versus what you can't. Practice acting on what's controllable and letting go of what's not.
- Turn your negative statements into questions: I'm terrible at interviewing. I'm terrible at interviewing? Are you? Always? What evidence do you have to support that statement? Scared is not the same as unskilled, and if you are unskilled, skill up! Take a class, get a coach, or read a book. (I recommend this one.)
- Failure isn't an end; it's the ultimate new beginning. You make a choice and it doesn't work out. Great! Put it on the list of what not to do, and try again. Resilience means realizing there must be more than one way to get where you want to go. To be courageous, you must keep going until you find it.
- Women often feel like they don't belong because we exist in a system that was created to keep up out. This feeling isn't limited to just a few women. In a KPMG poll of 750 high-performance, executive women, 75 percent had experienced imposter syndrome at some point during their career.
- To combat Impost-Her Syndrome, speak to yourself like you would your best friend, pinpoint how you're feeling without inflating or denying what happened, and remind yourself that you are not alone. Even the most influential and successful women have experienced failure. Ask yourself: What's the worst that can happen? Do I have the support and skills to deal with that? What have I learned from this experience? Readjust as necessary and proceed.

Chapter 7

The Three Commandments for Conquering Fear

Commandment #1—Prime

If you've read this far and completed the exercises, you are well on your way to creating a strong, clear, healthy voice that is authentically yours. Congratulations! Now it's time to put that voice to work.

The next three chapters are devoted to my Three Commandments for Conquering Fear: Prime, Pinpoint, and Power. The skills presented in these chapters build upon one another, so you'll want to complete the exercises chronologically. As a working mom of two little girls, if I'm going to devote some of my precious free time to something, it better be effective and it better be efficient. So the goal of these chapters is to help you conquer your fears about speaking, personally and professionally, as quickly and easily as possible.

To do this, I'll use the latest research on how the brain learns, combined with my own personal experience working with performers; they don't call it "performance anxiety" for nothing. In less than twenty minutes a day you can harness the power of your voice. Think of how much more centered and confident you will be knowing that regardless of situation, you can speak clearly and confidently, stay on (or get back on) track, relax your body, and be heard.

Let's get started.

Doing the Work

It has never been more important, more imperative, for women to speak up, to lead, to stop setting the table and take their seat at the head of it. It doesn't matter if you speak your truth on a national stage, at work, or at home. What matters is that your truth is spoken clearly and concisely, in a voice that is both stable and sustainable. What matters is that those around you, whether at the conference table or the kitchen table, connect with you and your message so your words aren't only heard, they're savored and remembered.

Truth time: Getting from shaking legs and sweaty palms to cool, calm, and collected is going to take more than watching inspirational videos about confidence on TikTok. To be clear, I see nothing wrong with this practice. I have spent many evenings seeking out solid life and parenting advice via TikTok. I am a huge fan of the dad whose son wouldn't stop playing video games, so he took the games out into the yard and ran his lawn mower over them. He is goals. But, if *you* want to create change, you're going to have to stop watching and start working. Let's start at the very beginning. I hear it's a pretty good place to start.

Prime means practice, because "winging it" is for the birds. In *Talk Like TED: The 9 Public Speaking Secrets of the World's Top Minds*, author Carmine Gallo interviews Dr. Pascal Michelon of Washington University in St. Louis on the topic of neuroplasticity, or the actual ability of the brain to grow and change over the course of a lifetime. Michelon says the areas of the brain that help us speak and articulate ideas clearly become more effective and efficient the more they are used.[1] The more you speak up, the more your brain literally changes and grows to make you a more effective speaker.

Prime also means preparing your brain to do her best work. In *The New Science of Learning: How to Learn in Harmony with Your Brain*, coauthor Terry Doyle (Hi, Dad!) discusses how the findings in neuroscience over the last decade have led to a new paradigm concerning how we learn. The brain can be prepared (primed, if you will) to learn, and doing so will increase the learner's chances for success.[2]

I really could have used this information in high school math class, where I "bagled" (to use the teacher's term) a quiz. That's right, Big Rapids High School Advanced Algebra fall of 1999—it was me. I got zero questions correct. As I'm now a university program head who consults internationally and is working on her first (soon to be best-selling) book, I can say without a shred of embarrassment that I did not then, and do not now, have any idea how to solve advanced algebraic equations.

To do her best work, your brain needs these five things: sleep, oxygen, exercise, hydration, and food (glucose).[3] If these sound like the basic "eat your veggies," "turn off the TV and go outside," tenets of mom-prescribed self-care—you're right, they are. They are also the first things to go out the window when you get busy.

Imagine this scenario: You were up late last night finishing a presentation, so you wake up exhausted. You grab a cup of coffee and head to work, where you sit at your desk all morning, getting up only once to pee and get another cup of coffee. When you finally decide to grab lunch, a colleague calls you into her office. You sit and talk, and before you know it, it's time for your afternoon meeting. You finish work, pick up your kids, drive home, and realize (as you're trying to figure out what you can feed your children in the twenty-seven minutes before your daughter's soccer practice) that the handful of Cheez-Its you're currently shoveling into your mouth is the first food you've had to eat all day. You end the night exhausted and have a glass (or three) of wine while watching the new season of *Housewives Battling in Tiaras* until after midnight because it's the only alone time you get all day before falling asleep and doing it all over again six hours later.

Sound familiar? I know it is for me. Running late in the morning? There goes breakfast. Didn't finish something for work or want a moment for myself? My free time sans kids is from 8:00 p.m. until I cannot keep my eyelids open. I regularly open a book I was reading the night before and have no idea what happened on the last three pages because I was falling asleep while reading. My exercise routine consists of two planned workouts per week and five days of chasing after my one-year-old, whose favorite habit is putting anything and everything from the kitchen floor into her mouth, especially the dog's treats, which I let her do because they keep her from screaming and I'm pretty sure they're not poisonous as the dog is still alive.

In 2019, I conducted a research study asking students in the performing arts at my university about their time-usage habits: basically, how much time they spent sleeping, studying, and rehearsing and when/what they were eating and drinking, particularly caffeine. I was interested not only in how students were prioritizing their time but also if they had any awareness of the consequences of their choices.

The results of the study confirmed my assumptions that the students weren't prioritizing the things that would positively impact their academic, creative, and personal well-being and they didn't have any real idea about the consequences of their decisions. I shared my study at a faculty meeting, and my colleagues responded similarly. Perhaps the lack of basic self-care and brain-care and the consequences to one's physical, mental, and emotional well-being as well as academic and creative success may be more endemic than I previously thought.

If reading the last few pages made you feel seen (or attacked), I'm with you. Life can get crazy! Last week I got in an argument with my husband, woke up at midnight, still mad, and ate his leftover birthday cheesecake—all of it—just so he couldn't have any. Luckily, by following these research-driven tips and tricks, you can make positive changes to your voice, body, and brain effectively and efficiently. Let's dive in.

Sleep: It's about WAY More Than Beauty

Most people consider themselves to be an early bird, what sleep scientists refer to as a lark, or a night owl. Basically, if you like to go to bed early and do your best work in the morning, you're a lark. If you're more productive at night and like to sleep until noon, you're a night owl. I'm a natural night owl who has, over time and an extreme amount of purely survival-based retraining, become a lark. The participants in my research were almost evenly split on being larks and night owls; however, nearly 70 percent of them said they usually woke up between 6:00 and 8:00 a.m.

As a night owl, I would go to sleep around 1:00 or 2:00 a.m. and wake up around 9:00 or 10:00 the next morning. This fit my natural tendencies and also allowed me to get my eight hours of sleep per night. Yes, you need seven to nine hours of sleep each night. There is a subset of the population with a genetic mutation that allows them to function on less than that, but it's small—like one-in-four-million small.[4] So even if you think it's you, trust me, it's not. If you're going to bed like a night owl and waking up like a lark, you're not getting enough sleep.

Not getting enough sleep results in more than just eye bags and ordering your coffee with an extra shot. In his book *Why We Sleep*, Matthew Walker, professor of neuroscience and psychology at UC Berkeley and the director of its Sleep and Neuroimaging Lab, says that lack of sleep results in difficulty paying attention, maintaining concentration, and recalling information from memory. It also weakens the immune system and makes you more likely to participate in poor decision-making.[5]

Let's see which of these skills you want on point when preparing for and having/giving an important conversation or presentation. Paying attention? Check. It's fairly important to be able to focus on the task at hand and those you're talking to. Maintaining concentration? Check. It's awfully difficult to get your point across or persuade an audience when your mind keeps wandering. Memory? Double check. I'd rank remembering what you want to say at the top the skill list for successful speaking. To prime your brain for speaking success, be sure to get your zzz's.

Even one night of poor sleep has negative consequences. According to Chiara Cirelli and Giulio Tononi of the University of Wisconsin's Institute of Sleep and Consciousness, every single part of the brain is negatively affected by sleep deprivation.[6] The first part of the brain to be affected is the prefrontal cortex, which monitors our social behavior: We become moody, irritable, and less rational. My husband and I have had some truly iconic fights based solely on sleep deprivation. I think the most memorable was when our first daughter was a colicky newborn who wouldn't sleep. It climaxed with my husband launching a tomato at our bedroom door. I have no idea what started the fight or why he had a tomato, but I know it happened because for weeks afterward the door had a reddish, tomato-sized stain on it.

Lack of sleep results in being more dehydrated than normal. This is because the hormone vasopressin, which is responsible for regulating the body's fluid levels, doesn't have time to do its job.[7] Basically, when you're sleep deprived, you are more likely to be dehydrated and not realize it. You already know from chapter 1 how important hydration is to keeping your voice feeling and sounding its best; now you can add "brain health" to your list of reasons to stay hydrated.

Sleep quality also influences the voice: Poor sleep quality results in poor vocal quality.[8] Ever woken up after a night of poor sleep sounding like a whiskey troll? In an article for the *Journal of Voice*, Alison Bagnall, Jill Dorrian, and Adam Fletcher refer to that tired morning voice as sounding "croaky," "rough," and "flat," adding that lack of sleep results in recognizable, consistent, and measurable negative impacts on the voice.[9] To explore this, the researchers asked fifteen participants to go without sleep for twenty-four hours. During that time, the subjects periodically read a standard passage and had their voices evaluated, both by trained listeners and acoustically. The results of the study showed that not only did the listeners note a deterioration in the subjects' voices in terms of energy and brilliance but the acoustic analysis revealed that their pitch fell. Lack of sleep literally made the participants sound more "croaky," "flat," and "down."

Lack of sleep causes a whole lot of deterioration to your voice and your body, but it's great at raising one thing: your stress levels. Stress, anxiety, and depression are all worsened by sleep loss.[10] You are probably familiar with how stress shows up in your body. For me, it's mild digestive issues (made so much worse by my habit of stress-eating dairy), fidgeting with my fingers, and running my tongue over my front teeth. (The last two I was unaware of until meeting my husband and having them brought thoughtfully, and constantly, to my attention. Thanks, honey.)

Stress also shows up in your voice. Results from a survey assessing risk factors for voice problems at two major music conservatory programs in the United States found the effects of stress, made worse by sleep loss, to be the most significant contribution to vocal problems, even when the participants were otherwise taking care of their voices.[11] If speaking up stresses you out—and I'm assuming it does, as you're reading this book—you can drastically improve your ability to calm down, think clearly, remember what you want to say, and sound clear and energized by getting enough sleep.

Adequate sleep is also crucial for practice. Researchers agree that sleep plays a vital role in the creation of memories.[12] During sleep the brain goes through the information taken in during the day to decide what is important and needs to be filed away and what can be dumped. The really important stuff gets sent from the hippocampus, which has limited storage, to the unlimited storage of the prefrontal cortex; the rest is dumped to prepare for the next day's info.[13]

How does the brain determine what's important? Repetition and positive emotional outcome.[14] Repeating something gives it importance, whether it's truly important information or not. I know all the words to the opening song from *Blippi* not because it's important information (it's not) or because I want to (I most definitely do not), but because I've heard it literally hundreds of times.

Your brain also loves what is deemed "good" for you. When you're excited and passionate about something your brain is like, "Sign me up!" This is another reason why positive self-talk is so important. The constant reinforcement that your conversation/presentation is going to go well and lead to great things instructs your brain to file the information quickly and completely because it is vital!

You've Got to Move It, Move It

Your brain evolved to learn on the move. Early humans were constantly making decisions in unstable outdoor environments, and they were making them while moving.[15] In their book *Spark: The Revolutionary New Science of Exercise and the Brain*, authors John Ratey and Eric Hagerman note that exercise isn't only important, it's the single most important thing a person can do to improve their learning.[16] They go on to say that exercise increases the production of neurotransmitters that boost focus and concentration, attention, motivation, patience, and your mood.

Like getting enough sleep, the concept that exercise is important to physical and mental health isn't a new one. I credit getting through the pandemic, during much of which I was pregnant and my husband and I were both working from home while caring for our three-year-old, without having a total mental breakdown to the forty-five minutes I spent every day on my spin bike (and crying in the shower).

In addition to its physical manifestations, acute stress causes the body to release hormones that get in the way of the brain's collecting and storing of memories.[17] This is not so great when you're trying to, say, memorize your talking points for an interview or sales pitch. Exercise does the opposite, actually causing neurons to grow and enhancing brainpower. Exercise produces brain-derived neurotrophic factor (BDNF), which is like Miracle-Gro for the brain, improving brain health, reducing stress, and making brain cells more resilient.[18]

To prime your brain for practice, you need to make exercise part of your weekly routine. I'm not saying you have to run a marathon or join a CrossFit gym. According to neuroscientist Wendy Suzuki, thirty minutes per day, most days of the week, will do it. Suzuki says she tries to do three to four half-hour workout sessions per week and focuses on aerobic exercise because it is the most brain beneficial, increasing heart rate and pumping more oxygen to the brain.[19]

Want to memorize information faster? Move. A huge part of being a performer is line and music memorization. It's awfully hard to give a compelling acting performance if you can't remember what comes next in the story. When my students ask me for help with this skill, I always tell them the same thing: Move. Don't break a sweat, but walk while you're memorizing. Even better, walk and speak your lines out loud. The first thing I do when working on a new script, for a play or a professional presentation, is get on the treadmill.

When I was finishing my master's, the final academic hurdle was the exit exam. This exam consisted of two complex essay questions from the student's field of study. One of mine was something like, "Give the history of opera from its beginnings to present day." We were all given our questions a month in advance but were not allowed to use notes on the day of the exam, which lasted four hours, had to be passed to graduate, and was notorious for taking students multiple attempts. As exam day approached, the anxiety among the graduate students in the school of music was palpable.

As I mentioned before, I went back to graduate school after working as an actress for a decade. I may not have known anything about music theory (though, thanks to my excellent paper-writing and presentation skills, I still squeaked by with a passing grade), but I knew how to memorize lines. I decided to treat my exit exam questions the same way. I wrote my answers out and went about memorizing them like a monologue. For me, that meant many, many early mornings spent walking circles in my yard while reading my answers aloud. If anyone driving by wondered what the woman at 8075 Burlingame was doing walking in circles and muttering to herself while wearing a bathrobe and being closely followed by a German Shepherd, they didn't ask.

A month of walking and talking later, I could recite my answers front, back, and sideways. I walked into the computer lab on the day of the exam, sat down, and typed my answers out as if I was reading them off the page. It took me just over an hour. The next week, one of my friends told me that my quick exam finish was a point of major conversation among the graduate students. How did she do it? Sorcery? No, science.

Eat, Drink, and Be Heard

Your brain functions a lot like the rest of your body: If she's hungry and thirsty, she's not in the greatest mood or doing her best work. Water is essential for brain health. Neurons—the cells in the brain and nervous system that send and receive messages from the outside world—actually take in and store water in tiny balloon-like structures called vacuoles.[20] Dehydration impairs the brain's short-term and long-term memory function (your ability to make new memories and recall old ones).[21] Your mood, ability to think clearly, and energy levels are all affected by even slight dehydration.[22]

Your brain also needs energy, and just like your muscles, it gets that energy from the food you eat. Your brain requires twenty-two times the amount of energy to run as the equivalent weight in muscle tissue.[23] And you'd better feed her right: Everything from learning to memory to our mood and emotions is directly affected by the food we eat.[24]

Your brain needs a diet full of healthy fats, protein, and carbohydrates. About 60 percent of the brain's solid matter is fat. These mostly polyunsaturated fats keep brain cell membranes flexible, which aids the cells' ability to communicate. To keep your brain fat and happy, be sure to include plenty of omega-3 fats in your diet: fish, dark leafy greens, seeds, and nuts. You'll also want to include omega-6 fats like corn, safflower, and borage oils.[25]

Notice I did not mention Oreos, french fries, or ice cream in my list of brain-healthy fats. Trans and saturated fats do not count in your quest for brain health. I know, I'm sad too. These fats are super dangerous because they can take the place of the healthy polyunsaturated fats in your brain cell membranes, making the membranes stiff and prohibiting cell communication. They can also prevent oxygen from getting into your brain and waste from getting out of it.

Serotonin and dopamine, two of the well-known "feel-good" neurotransmitters in the brain, both rely on protein. Serotonin calms you down, while dopamine lifts your energy and your mood.[26] I don't know about you, but when I'm going into an important conversation, personally or professionally, I want to calm my anxiety and feel good about what's going to happen.

Wearing a great outfit and smiling like you mean it (even when you don't) are fine, but if I can actually get my brain to release the neurotransmitters whose job it is to (1) calm me down and (2) lift my mood, I'm there. Especially when it's as easy as including more healthy proteins in my meals. This could look like swapping out your breakfast cereal for eggs or switching from peanut butter to almond butter on your toast. (Almonds have a much more brain-healthy combo of protein and fat than peanuts.)

Carbohydrates, specifically glucose (or sugar), are the main source of fuel for the brain. No other food source meets your brain's energy requirements.[27] You have no doubt felt the surge of energy that comes with eating a shit ton of simple carbs, and if you have, you've also experienced the drop in energy that comes once those carbs are used up. Because your brain requires glucose to function, she likes to have a steady supply. Enter complex carbohydrates.

Complex carbohydrates are often found in foods that are highly nutritious, like brown rice, barley, oats, and buckwheat. Compared to simple carbs, the molecules that make up complex carbohydrates are longer, so they take more time for the body to process, thus providing longer-lasting energy.[28]

The best brain diet is one that is rich in all of these: healthy fats, protein, and complex carbohydrates. By incorporating these into your diet, you are not only keeping your brain healthy, you're actually priming it to work more effectively and efficiently.

Practice, Practice, Practice

One of the keys to being a great speaker is being able to pause, answer a question, or rearrange your points on the fly to best serve the moment and the audience. To do this, you must know your material cold. No exceptions. Reading word for word from a note card or PowerPoint isn't going to cut it. Snooze fest! And what if you lose your place? Insert awkward pause here while you desperately try to find where you left off and your audience grabs their phones because pictures of fat babies who look like their pets are suddenly much more interesting than whatever it is you're trying to talk about.

Often clients are worried about memorizing their material and coming off sounding robotic, to which I say, "If you sound like a robot, you don't know your stuff well enough." You need to become an expert on whatever it is you are talking about. You need to make it your passion, your purpose, your jam. The good news is, since you're working on changing your life, there's a good chance it already is.

With that passion comes research. You have to do the work. You can be as excited about opening a bakery as my five-year-old daughter on Christmas morning, but that means nothing to a potential investor if you don't have a detailed plan for what you're going to do with their money.

I have a student who is like sunshine. She is lovely in just about every way someone can be lovely. It is a joy to have her in class each week. She's caring, genuine, and so charming she could sell sand in the Sahara. I failed her last semester. Why? Because she didn't turn in the final project that accounted for 50 percent of her grade. She just didn't do it, and no matter how much I like her or how highly I think of her, I could not give her credit for work she did not do. You have to do the work.

Try this: Think about your favorite movie, the movie you could watch on any day of the week and enjoy it. If movies aren't your thing, substitute your favorite book/dessert/song/whatever; the point is that it is something near and dear to your heart. Now tell me all about it. Tell me who stars in it and what the story is. Tell me who wrote the script and how it differs from the book. Tell me about the director and how you like all her movies, but this is your favorite. Tell me about your favorite scene, your favorite lines, your favorite scenery and costumes. Tell me about the behind-the-scenes bloopers, the cameos, the scene that got cut but you can still find on a back channel of YouTube. Tell me the details you notice that no one else cares about.

See what happens? See how you can talk, in detail, about this movie with ease because you know what happens in each scene and you've memorized every line? See how you're smiling when you talk about your favorite moments? Does it make you want to go and turn it on right now? I hope so. That's how you need to talk about your topic, answer your interview questions, persuade your investor, whatever. You need to know things that only true fans know, things that no one else knows. Your passion is in the details.

SUMMARY

- Prime means practice. It also means preparing your brain to do her best work. Brain science research over the last decade tells us that your brain can be primed to learn and that doing so will increase your chance for success.
- Your brain needs these five things to thrive: sleep, oxygen, exercise, hydration, and food (glucose).
- These five things may sound like the basic "eat your veggies" tenets of self-care, and they are, but they're also often the first things to go out the window when you get busy.
- Sleep is about way more than beauty. Even one poor night of sleep (less than seven hours) makes you more irritable, anxious, and stressed. Lack of sleep also makes it more difficult to pay attention, maintain concentration, and recall information from memory.
- During sleep, your brain determines which information from the previous day is important and needs to be held onto and which can be dumped to make room for the next day's info. To be sure your brain puts your upcoming speech into the "keep" folder, it's a great idea to practice just before bed and first thing when you wake up in the morning.
- Your brain loves repetition. She also loves positive emotional connection or things that are deemed "good" for you. This is why both practice and positive self-talk are both so important. When you're constantly reinforcing how passionate and excited you are about something, you're telling your brain, "This is important!"

- Your brain evolved to learn on the move. Exercise, especially aerobic exercise, is necessary for brain health. Exercise increases attention, concentration, and motivation, and it makes you happier. It also makes your brain more able to make and store memories.
- My number-one tip for learning and memorizing anything new? Move. Get on the treadmill or walk circles in your yard while reading and talking out loud. You'll learn the info quicker and get your steps in. Win-win.
- Your brain, like your body, needs to be well fed and hydrated. Otherwise, she gets hangry. The best diet for your brain is full of healthy fats, protein, and complex carbohydrates, which will keep your brain happy with a steady stream of fuel.
- Great speakers know that "winging it" is for the birds. You need to make your words your purpose, your passion, your jam. Get to know them up, down, and sideways so you can speak them the same way you'd talk about your favorite movie. Your passion is in the details.

Chapter 8

Commandment #2—Pinpoint

Pinpoint means focus. This chapter is all about helping you develop the ability to focus on your message, regardless of what else is happening. I'm going to help you prepare not for what *will* happen but for what *could* happen. You could hit traffic and be running late. A cell phone could go off while you're speaking. You could be asked an unexpected question. Your spouse could glance at your computer screen on his shirtless walk from the bathroom to the Keurig, see you in a Zoom with what looks like only your good friend but is actually the entire faculty and staff of your department, and bellow, "Hey dipshit! Looking sexy, my man!" (Trust me, it could happen.)

Fear of losing focus is usually rooted in the fear of the unknown. Uncertainty is part of life; some people thrive in uncertain times, while others get deer-in-the-headlights paralyzed. The psychological term for fear of the unknown is "xenophobia."[1] Currently, the term is usually associated with the fear of strangers, but its original definition encompasses anything or anyone that is unknown or uncertain. It's fear of the "what if."

If you're anything like me, "what if" can start off in a really basic, true-to-life, this-could-actually-happen place and quickly snowball into more of a nuclear war, spontaneous combustion, end-of-the-world place. When I was first working with my therapist, I explained to her that I had a fear of being alone, especially at night, and that this fear evolved into not only the spontaneous purchase of an elaborate alarm system but also me literally taking a power drill and screwing our windows shut one night when my husband was gone on a business trip. I remember her thanking me for my honesty and awarding me both an assignment of daily meditation and a prescription for Zoloft.

Fear of the unknown is often caused by a situation's lack of predictability and your lack of control over it. Speaking, whether professional or personal, is chock-full of both. The reality is that you don't know exactly what's going to happen in a presentation or conversation. You might have a good idea, particularly if this isn't your first time with these people or at this venue, but you don't know for sure. You don't know how your audience is going to respond. The joke that worked the week before might fall flat. The job your boss has been hinting at giving you for the last six months might go to someone else. The object of your affection might say no.

If just reading these words has got you sweating, take a deep breath before this next part: You have no control over any of it. You have no control over what your audience finds funny. You have no control over whether your heart's desire wants to be with you or whether your boss sees you as the best person for the job. Instead of letting this lack of control frustrate you, look at it as a gift. It's the gift of freedom, of having zero fucks to give, of being able to say, "It's not me; it's you," all neatly wrapped in a colorful package with a sparkly bow.

But what if you want your audience to find you funny? What if you want the job? What if you want to be with this person? If you have no control over the outcome, why are you even trying? You're trying because even though you ultimately can't control someone else's feelings or decision, you can be damn sure to do everything in your power to persuade them. You can absolutely, 100 percent control how prepared you are. You can research your audience so you know what they find funny and what they find offensive. You can organize your material in a way that makes it most effective, bribe your friends and family with snacks so they'll watch you practice and give you feedback, and then take that feedback and adjust, then adjust again. You can also practice reacting to the unexpected so that even though you might not know what will happen, you do know how to keep going.

The following exercises are great to do once you've memorized what you want to say. (If you need help memorizing, head back to chapter 7.) Being really comfortable with what you want to say is important, whether you're giving a presentation or having an important conversation. You can control whether you say everything you want to, so make learning your material your number-one concern.

Fear and anxiety often show up physically: dry mouth, shaking legs, sweaty palms, shortness of breath, and rapid heartbeat. These symptoms show up when the sympathetic nervous system is activated, and it can be scary. It can also make delivering your words with authenticity and personality seem impossible.

Each year, I teach a course to the entire class of musical theatre freshmen called Intro to Musical Theatre Voice. We cover a lot of what's in this book: breathing, posture, basic vocal anatomy, and vocal health. We also cover dealing with performance anxiety. Even under the best of circumstances, speaking (and singing) in front of other people can be scary. When my students complain about how scary and uncomfortable it is to be up in front of the group, I remind them of two things: (1) this is something you chose to pursue because it's getting you closer to your goals and (2) when it's uncomfortable, that's when growth happens.

Skill Up: Embracing Uncomfortable

I have a drawing tacked to the corkboard in my office. It's of a timeline that starts with "comfort," then hits "discomfort," and finally ends in "pain." The line between "comfort" and "discomfort" is relatively short, but the line between "discomfort" and "pain" is long. It's something I use with my students a lot. After a new or particularly taxing exercise I usually ask, "On a scale of 1 to 10, how was that? One is 'That felt great; let's do it again,' and 10 is 'My throat is bleeding.'" Then I tell them that I'm okay with continuing until that number starts to reach about a 7 or 8. At a 7 or 8, it's definitely not comfortable, but it's not yet painful. An 8 tells me this is the last time we should do this today.

I like to assign number values because it allows students to really see their growth. What starts out as an 8 during the first week of the month is often closer to a 5 by month's end. Once the exercise is consistently hitting a 2 or a 3, it's time to find a new challenge.

I'm going to ask you to use the same scale for the following exercises. In this case, we're not gauging physical pain so much as fear response. In this case, 1 would be something like, "I feel totally comfortable. I've got my act together; let's take it on the road," and 10 would be more like "A slow, painful death is imminent."

Each of the things listed below is a common "what if" fear when it comes to speaking. To prepare your body, mind, and voice for what *could* happen, I'm going to ask you to re-create various physical responses your body has to that fear. Then you're going to practice giving your talk while experiencing this response. The more you do it, the easier it becomes to work through it.

Sweaty palms, shortness of breath, and a racing heart are all hallmarks of an acute stress response that wreaks havoc on memory retrieval. When stressed, the brain shifts into memory formation mode and out of memory retrieval mode, making it more difficult to retrieve memories unrelated to the cause of the stress.[2] This makes total sense in the survival-based big picture—your brain's main concern mid–bear attack shouldn't be your upcoming venture capital pitch—but it's a problem when the stress you're responding to is less bear attack and more bumper-to-bumper traffic on the freeway.

You might remember from chapter 2 that turning off the fight-or-flight response of the sympathetic nervous system and turning on the rest-and-digest of the parasympathetic nervous system takes about an hour. What do you do when it's "go time" and your body is still in panic mode? If you don't have time to calm down, you're going to have to learn how to speak when you're scared. Treat it like learning to do anything else: The more you do it, the more skilled you will become. In the words of the great Meryl Streep, "Do it alone. Do it broke. Do it tired. Do it scared. Just do it!"[3]

The scenario: You left your house with plenty of time to drive the thirty miles to your interview, which, last night, Google Maps told you would take thirty-seven minutes to complete. Now, thanks to an accident, you're creeping along the freeway at a snail's pace. You call the company to let them know, and then, rather than being unforgivably late, decide to exit the freeway and take the side streets, which you have never driven before.

Twenty minutes and three U-turns later, you arrive at the parking lot, jump out of your car, slam the door, and sprint up the two flights of stairs to the correct office because there is no time to wait for the elevator. By the time you arrive at the reception desk, you're sweaty and out of breath, and your heart is halfway through the drum solo from "Wipe Out." The receptionist greets you warmly and says that the interview team is ready for you; please go in now.

The work: Try the following. The goal is to be short of breath with an elevated heart rate, so adjust times and intensity accordingly.

- Do jumping jacks, run up and down stairs, or run in place for one minute, then give your talk.

- Walk quickly around your house or office, like you're running late and looking for the correct room, then give your talk.

The scenario: You've finally landed a meeting with your dream venture capital firm and are ready to pitch them your start-up. You walk into the boardroom, where five people are seated around a table. They introduce themselves as the firm's bigwigs, and you shake hands. You hand out your glossy marketing materials and power up your slides, but just as you're ready to start speaking your legs begin to shake. Your mouth goes dry. Your palms sweat. The head bigwig asks you to begin whenever you're ready, and you can't remember how to start.

The work:

- Stand with your back against a sturdy, flat wall. Walk your feet out a foot or two and slide down the wall until your knees are bent at a 90-degree angle to the floor, as if you're sitting in a chair. Hold this position until your legs feel like noodles and your heart rate is elevated, then give your talk.
- Do push-ups (on your knees, your toes, or against a wall) until your arms feel like noodles and your heart rate is elevated, then give your talk.
- If you have a set of dumbbells, you can use these here; two canned goods of the same size will work also. Standing with your feet shoulder width apart, hold one dumbbell in each hand, and, bending your elbows, bring them up to your shoulders. Squat down till the tops of your thighs are parallel to the floor (or as far as is comfortable), then, as you stand back up, push the dumbbells up over head till your biceps are by your ears. Repeat until your arms and legs are noodle-esque and your heart rate is elevated, then give your talk.

The scenario: You're in the middle of a presentation and it's going great! You've hit all your talking points and have your audience in the palm of your hand—until someone's cell phone goes off, an assistant walks in, someone starts hacking up a lung, or you're asked an unrelated question. Pick your poison. The unexpected disturbance derails your train of thought and you're struggling to get it back on the tracks.

The work: Grab a partner or two. Set up a space that mimics the one you'll be in for the real deal. Give your partners each a notepad and pen and have them open a door (or a pretend door) to invite you into the room. Try to make this as close to real life as possible. Start your talk and have your partner:

- Call your cell phone so it rings at unexpected times.
- Have one person with you in the room and the other barge in late, or start your talk to a pretend audience and have your partner walk in part way through.
- Have your partner start coughing.
- Have them ask unrelated questions.

The more (realistic) disturbances, the better. Practice maintaining your focus and continuing your talk after each interruption.

After each exercise, rate yourself on a scale of 1 to 10 with 1 being "That went perfectly" and 10 being "That was the worst ever." If your rating is higher than you'd like it to be (I suggest aiming for 2 and below), try repeating this exercise daily for a week, then rate yourself again.

The Somatic Rolodex

During the summer of 2021, I was asked by SpeakOut Revolution, a UK-based nonprofit whose mission is to cancel the culture of silence on harassment and bullying in our workplaces, to cohost a workshop on gaslighting. I was paired with a mindset coach who was going to speak to the internal work needed to recognize and combat gaslighting, while I was talking about the actual how-to of speaking up.

I was really excited for the opportunity. SpeakOut had just been awarded the UK Gold Business Award for Diversity and Inclusion and was in the trenches making positive changes to workplace culture for women. I spent weeks preparing my presentation: fine-tuning my slides and practicing what I was going to say. I researched statistics on gaslighting in the workplace and read countless articles on the topic to make sure I would be able to answer any question that was asked.

The presentation, via Zoom, went off without a hitch. The mindset coach presented her material, and then it was my turn. I started as I usually do, showing a picture of me, age eight, wearing a white satin leotard with a white lace train and matching hat, the costume for my performance of Madonna's "Vogue" in the Miss Janine's School of Dance annual dance recital. I talked about my background as a performer and how that grew into teaching, research, and writing. I use the photo because it's cute, funny, and puts everyone at ease, which is especially helpful when the topic we're discussing is as emotionally fraught as gaslighting is.

I talked about identifying gaslighting, how to speak up against it, and the reality that speaking up garners reactions that aren't always positive. The audience was engaged, asked great questions, and had positive feedback afterward. All in all, I felt things went exactly as I wanted them to go. A win.

Then I watched the video back. As I thought, my content was great. What wasn't so great was my delivery. Each time I paused during my talk I pressed my tongue to the roof of my mouth and then pulled it down, resulting in a little sucking noise, like the noise my grandmother used to make when she'd catch me biting my nails: "Stsk, stsk, stsk." I did this every single time I paused, and because I was breathing deeply, pacing myself, and watching my audience for questions, I paused a lot.

I was totally embarrassed. Here I was, the expert on speaking, and I made this annoying noise during my entire presentation. I was immediately convinced that I would never be hired again by SpeakOut or anyone else. How did I not know I was doing this?

Upon further reflection, I realized that it wasn't, in fact, the end of the world. I was still a pretty good speaker, and there was at least a chance I wouldn't lose my career, be abandoned by my family, and wander the earth desperate and alone until freezing to death one long winter's night with my nose pressed desperately against the window of a Krispy Kreme. But seriously, how did I not know?

The answer to this lies in the Somatic Rolodex. The Somatic Rolodex is a catalogue of all the movements your body has done since birth.[4] Some of these movements serve you really well: a perfectly timed golf swing, a well-sung high note, lifting with the legs and not with the back once you're over thirty. Some don't serve you as well, but the Somatic Rolodex doesn't distinguish between the two, it just makes the movements available. Sometimes habits develop that include movements that aren't so great for you, and once those habits are in place, they're really hard to break.

Apparently, the annoying little sucking noise I was using to replace the need to say "Um" was a well-formed habit in my Somatic Rolodex—a very well-formed habit, as I was so used to doing it, I had no idea it was happening.

This all could have been prevented had I even once videoed myself while I was practicing. Setting up my phone to record or Zooming with myself and recording that meeting would have alerted me to my habit and given me the chance to fix it. I was so sure of myself, my experience, and my skills that I failed to take one of my own most common pieces of advice: Get yourself on film.

Way back in chapter 4 I had you video yourself speaking to evaluate your voice and your progress, so by now, you're hopefully more comfortable with the practice. Even if you're not, trust me: Seeing yourself on film, even if you're not having a great hair day and forgot to wax your chin, is so much better than waiting until you're in front of an audience to find out that you like to chew your bottom lip, or gesticulate with only your left hand, or make a stupid sucking noise with your tongue after every damn sentence.

All the scenarios and exercises above are geared at making your practice more effective. You're skilling up on embracing the uncomfortable and remaining focused in the face of uncertainty. You can't predict the future, but you can be really, really prepared to handle whatever the universe decides to throw at you. Now let's focus on making your practice more efficient, because your time is precious.

Skill Up: Master It Faster

Last night, my husband was sitting at the dinner table on his computer typing an email while I was simultaneously cooking dinner and telling him about a phone call I had with a friend who was thinking of buying a house. The conversation went something like this:

Me: Rebecca and Trent are thinking of buying a house.

My husband: Uh-huh. (keeps typing)

Me: I told her I really think they should wait. The market is just so expensive right now. What do you think?

My husband: Uh-huh.

Me: Uh-huh, what? Do you think they should buy a place, or do you think they should wait?

My husband: Uh-huh.

Me: I'm pregnant with Jason Momoa's baby.

My husband: Uh-huh.

Me: Aliens have landed and are abducting our neighbors.

My husband: Uh-huh.

Me: Your daughter just took a shit on the floor.

My husband: Wait—what?!

Obviously, my husband wasn't listening because men never listen and he doesn't care about what happened during my day, right? Wrong. My husband wasn't listening because when I started talking, he was already engaged in another task, and his brain is a terrible multitasker. Guess what? So is yours.

Many of the women I know consider themselves to be excellent multitaskers. It's often a source of pride. There's a stereotype that women are better multitaskers than men, which, according to Leah Ruppanner, associate professor of sociology and codirector of the Policy Lab at the University of Melbourne, in an article in *Science Alert*, is just not true. The article is titled "Women Are Not Better at Multitasking, They Just Do More Work."[5] Damn, Leah.

Ruppanner cites a study out of the Melbourne Institute for Applied Economic and Social Research that studied the hours per week of housework done by each member of a male/female couple, where both parties were employed, over the course of two years. The study found that regardless of who the breadwinner was or if the earnings were equal, the majority of the housework was done by the women.

While it might seem like women are master multitaskers as they balance their own careers with coordinating childcare, planning and cooking meals, making doctor's appointments, and keeping the house from looking like a nuclear bomb went off, they're not. They're just really fucking overworked.

What happens when you try to multitask? Like my husband, who couldn't pay attention to his email and my questions at the same time, the two (or more) things you're wanting to do are constantly at war for your attention. The architecture of the human brain, the building blocks that make up our mental functions, are not set up to do more than one task at a time, so you're constantly switching between the tasks, leaving one unfinished to do the other.[6]

The result? Attempting to complete multiple tasks at the same time takes longer than completing each task individually. I know this to be true because as I've been writing this chapter, I've also been checking my phone to see if my daughters' daycare has updated their Brightwheel app, checking Facebook to see if anyone liked my recent post (because I will pull it down if not; I'm that shallow), drinking a quad-shot latte, and answering emails about my upcoming workshop—all of which resulted in it taking an hour to write the previous three paragraphs, which should have taken me fifteen minutes.

In addition to telling your partner to start doing their own damn laundry, here's how you can use this information to benefit your practice.

The scenario: You've carved out thirty minutes from your day to practice for your upcoming talk. You're well fed and hydrated, got eight glorious hours of sleep the night before, and are all set up to record your session. You press "record" and begin. It goes okay—not the best, but better than you hoped. You watch it back and realize that you forgot your second point, you're saying "you know" too much, and your left hand seems to have a mind of its own.

The work: Begin your practice session the same way, by recording your talk all the way through without stopping. Don't worry about making mistakes; just keep going. Be careful of getting in the habit of stopping when you make a mistake. Remember, your brain loves repetition, and what you don't want is to get in the habit of stopping every time something doesn't go the way you want it to.

Next, go back and watch the recording and write down everything you'd like to fix. If you're just starting out in the process, focus on the big things: making sure you got all your talking points in order, you didn't leave out any important information, and you're completely comfortable with everything you're saying. Once you've got those down, then you can focus on the smaller things: your gestures, any habits that aren't serving you, if you need to speak louder or softer, and fine-tuning a joke or story.

Once you've made your "Needs Improvement" list, divide the rest of your practice time into segments. If you're practicing for thirty minutes, then three ten-minute segments might work well, but adjust accordingly. Assign one "fix" to each segment. Then, for the rest of that segment, focus only on that one thing. At the end of that segment, move on to the next "fix."

When your thirty minutes are up, rerecord the entire talk. You can either watch it back right then, so you have notes for your next practice session, or start your next session with it. Whatever serves you and your time best.

The Importance of Multisensory Learning

Your brain learns faster when you use more of your senses. The more parts of the brain that are activated, the better chance you have of remembering things and connecting the new information to what you already know.[7]

I'm going to share with you a story my dad uses when he presents research on how the brain learns. Imagine you live in a house, and near that house is a lake. Every day you walk to the lake, and you take the same path through the woods. The path gets really worn, and you get to know it so well you could walk it with your eyes closed. Then one night there's a storm and a tree falls, blocking the path. How do you get to the lake?

The story is based on the house I grew up in, which is near a lake and has a path through the woods. This actually happened when I was in high school, so I know the answer, which is that you call your ultra-hunky neighbor, who brings over his chainsaw, and then watch his Wrangler-clad ass as he clears the tree out of the path before offering him a cool glass of lemonade and your virginity. (I'm kidding, Mom.)

The more senses you use, the more paths to the lake you have, so to speak, and the quicker you'll be able to get there.

The scenario: You have an in-person interview for your dream job. To prepare, you sit down to work out your answers to the questions you'll likely be asked. You write your answers down and then read them to yourself silently for twenty minutes. When your partner comes home, you channel the advice in this chapter and ask them to practice with you by asking you the questions, but you struggle to remember your answers.

The work: Start with writing your answers down, but instead of reading them to yourself, read aloud and record your answers into a voice memo on your phone. Then take both your phone and your written answers outside, or hop on the treadmill, and walk at a leisurely pace while you both listen to the recording and read along. In your next practice sessions, as you get to know the answers better, ditch the paper and speak the answers aloud with only the recording, then ditch the recording. Once you're ready, trade walking for sitting as you will at the interview, and then have a partner ask you the questions so you can answer them in real time.

The multisensory approach also carries over into giving a presentation or speech. If you want your audience to connect and remember your material, involve their senses. Rather than just standing at a podium talking, ask active questions, have your audience ask their neighbors questions, toss a tennis ball and have audience members answer or ask a question once they've caught it. In my classroom, I ditched test review from a book and instead play trivia games that get my students talking to each other and moving around the classroom. My favorite thing is tossing candy when I ask review questions—literally throwing a little sugar at the problem.

Summary

- Pinpoint means focus. The goal is to be able to focus on your words regardless of what else is going on around you.
- Fear of losing focus is usually rooted in the fear of the unknown, the "what if." This fear is often caused by a situation's lack of predictability and your lack of control over it. Speaking, personally and professionally, is chock-full of both.
- Try looking at your lack of control as a gift of freedom, of having zero fucks to give, of being able to say, "It's not me; it's you," all neatly wrapped in a colorful package with a sparkly bow. You can't control someone else's feelings or decision, but you can 100 percent control how prepared you are to persuade them.
- When the symptoms of fear show up, it can be scary. It can also make delivering your words with authenticity and personality seem impossible. Instead of thinking how scary and uncomfortable it is to be up in front of a group, remind yourself of two things: (1) this is something you chose to pursue because it's getting you closer to your goals and (2) when things are uncomfortable is when growth happens.
- It takes an hour for your parasympathetic rest-and-digest system to kick in, which means that sometimes, you're going to have to do it scared. By re-creating the body's physical reactions to fear, you can learn how to remain focused and in the moment, even when something unexpected happens.
- Record yourself on video. You have habits and physical tics that are so ingrained you may not even be aware of them.

Always, always get yourself on video so you can see and hear what you actually look and sound like.

- Your brain is a terrible multitasker. The human brain evolved to focus on one task at a time. When you try to focus on more than one, a war for focus starts where the only one losing is you. To prepare for your talk faster, divide your practice session into sections and focus on one "fix" at a time.
- Use all your senses. The more senses you use, the more of your brain activates, and the more of your brain that activates, the quicker you can learn new material and connect it to what you already know. Walk, read aloud, listen, write, and then, to keep your audience engaged, encourage them to do the same.

Chapter 9

Commandment #3—Power

During my second year of grad school, I decided to attend my first professional opera audition. I had spent the last eighteen months studying the art form and decided it was time to put my new skills to work. The audition was for a midsized company's production of *Rigoletto*, and there was a small role for a mezzo-soprano that my voice teacher said would be great for me.

The audition call asked for two pieces, which blew my freaking mind. To give you some background, the audition call for a musical theatre audition is usually one 16–32-bar cut, which equals about thirty seconds of music. It was rumored that at the open auditions for *The SpongeBob Musical* there were so many people auditioning that the casting team started asking for 8-bar cuts. That's like fifteen seconds of music. It's like taking Whitney Houston's "I Will Always Love You" and just singing "you."

On the day of the audition, I spent a couple of hours getting my hair and makeup just right and selected an outfit that I thought made me look like I knew what I was doing, which I absolutely did not. I arrived at the opera company and made my way to the holding room, which is the room where everyone who's waiting to sing sits, to sign in. The holding room was the size of a large office and had a wall of windows overlooking the audition space below, which I thought was great because I could sneak a peek at the singers who went before me and have an idea of what to expect.

As I was trying to appear at ease and simultaneously hold in the nervous gas that had formed in my gut and was now knock, knock, knocking on heaven's door, in walked Dr. LaToya Lain, one of the voice professors from my university, who is a serious, *serious* professional. She's sung all over the world, performed at the Met, and had recently finished singing at the L'Église Americaine a Paris (the American Church in Paris) as part of an event to commemorate Dr. Martin Luther King's 1964 visit. She was (and still is) a total boss. I wanted to be her when I grew up.

Seeing Dr. Lain was nice because at least I knew someone, and also terrifying because if she was at this audition, I was definitely way out of my league. She sang before me, and during her audition everyone in the holding room was like looking at each other like, "Who in the mother-loving hell is that?" I stood a little taller and whispered to the woman next to me, "That's Dr. LaToya Lain. Isn't she fantastic? She's at CMU . . . so am I." (LaToya, if you're reading this, yes, this really happened. I really did shamelessly coattail on your audition, and I really do still want to be you when I grow up.)

It was almost my turn, so I did what I usually do at auditions and took the nervous energy that starts out as, "Oh shit, it's almost my turn," and turned it into, "Let's go! When is it going to be my turn?" This practice works really well for me, and I highly recommend trying it. Before a big event, the nervous energy is going to be there, so you might as well channel it into something good. Plus, I'm really competitive, and thinking this way makes me feel like a sprinter on the starting block, waiting for the starter pistol to go off. (At least I imagine that's how a sprinter feels; I only run if being chased.)

My mindset shift started working, and when my name was called, I walked down the stairs and into the audition space thinking, "I am the best singer in this room." Which was technically true, as at that moment I was the only singer in the room. I got the "I'm the best in this room" from my first voice teacher, a good friend of my family who offered to give me voice lessons at the university where he taught when I was eleven. My mom would pick me up from school and we'd drive the thirty minutes to his office, where I'd strictly instruct her to wait in the car. I didn't want any of the college students thinking I was just a little kid, because clearly an eleven-year-old in a Catholic school uniform carrying a magenta JanSport backpack just screamed "collegiate."

I'd stand beside the piano while he played scales and instructed me to sing them back. Then he'd let me pick a song to work on, always from a Broadway musical. I'd usually pick something from *Phantom of the Opera* because I was obsessed with Sarah Brightman. At the end of the lesson, he'd hand me my music and say in his booming bass, "Remember, Jessica, when you walk into the room, you're the best goddamn singer in it, and don't let anyone, ever, tell you otherwise. Tell your dad I'll call him for golf next week."

I've kept that piece of advice with me and now share it with my students and clients. I'm not saying to act conceited, and I'm definitely not saying to share this thought with anyone else, but nothing feels quite as good as walking into a room like you own it. Besides, if you don't think you're the most qualified person in the room, how is anyone else supposed to?

I handed my music to the pianist and walked him through the tempo changes, then hit the "X" in the middle of the floor and gave my slate—fancy performer-speak for introducing myself and what I was going to sing. Then I lowered my head and took two deep breaths. When I lifted my head, the pianist started playing, and we were off.

This head-lowering, deep-breathing moment is my preaudition ritual. Like a basketball player shooting a free throw or a pitcher preparing to release a pitch, it's a short series of actions I take every single time I get up to audition. It's the moment when

I say to myself, "It's time." See, you can prepare and you can focus, but when it's time to do the damn thing, you have to do it!

The audition went well. The casting director even asked me to sing my second piece, which is always a good sign. Ultimately, I didn't get the job, but what I did do was decide to go after something that was outside my comfort zone and then go after it courageously, not holding anything back.

That's what this chapter is all about.

FINDING YOUR POWER

The last two chapters have been all about what comes before; this chapter is about what happens when the countdown ends. I am absolutely not going to tell you that you will be able to completely calm your nerves, because you won't. Frankly, if you're not at least a little bit nervous, then the stakes aren't high enough. I'm also not going to ask you to relax, because going after what you want is not a relaxed activity. Relaxing is sitting on the couch watching Netflix. I want you activated. I want you poised like the skier at the top of the mountain, not tense, but ready for all the twists and turns that will show up on your way down.

My dear friend Jessica Teague is a ballerina, internationally published writer, and professor of dance. She also has pet tigers. At dinner one night, the topic of if and when we'd met famous people came up. I said I'd once followed David Hasselhoff around at a mall in LA, my husband had met Detroit Lions football player Herman Moore at the airport, and Jessica nonchalantly said she'd danced for Vladimir Putin. The whole story was that as a member of the Dutch National Ballet, she was flown on the queen's private plane to Russia, where she danced in a private concert for the Russian president. She did this when she was like twenty.

I had to know more, including how she wasn't completely and totally terrified, especially at such a young age. That's when she told me about her tigers. Jessica said that whenever she goes into a situation where she's intimidated or afraid, she imagines she has a tiger walking on either side of her. I know—it's the most badass thing I've ever heard too. When Jessica is walking between her tigers, she lifts her chin a little higher, drops her shoulders down a little lower, and narrows her gaze a little more. She's unstoppable because no one messes with a bad bitch and her Bengals.

Maybe She's Born with It; Maybe It's Self-Efficacy

Where does courage come from, and why do some people just seem to be more courageous than others? How do Malala and Greta and Kamala and Glennon do what they do? Part of it is physical. Neuroscience research has determined that courageous people have a somewhat different brain structure than those who are more risk averse.[1] This structure, combined with a strong commitment to their values, could make it more likely that courageous people will choose to act even in the face of risk.

While anatomy may have something to do with it, courage is also attributed to self-efficacy, a term coined by psychologist Albert Bandura, meaning an individual's belief in their ability reach their goals.[2] Self-efficacy affects not only a person's belief in their own ability but also the subsequent choices they make.

My husband and I had been married about three years when we started talking about having a family. At that time, he was commuting an hour each way to work and I was running my vocal studio, which meant I was gone most nights and weekends. (If you've run a small business, particularly a service-based business, you know how hard it is to say no to a client when booking that client keeps the bills paid.)

Our lifestyle was not conducive to having kids, and frankly, I wasn't feeling particularly challenged at work. I've always been a go-getter, a goal-setter, a do-er. I returned home to Michigan after living in Los Angeles and decided to start my vocal studio, so I did. I found a space, emailed every high school choir and drama teacher in a sixty-mile radius, and took a "day job" in a daycare that involved both getting up before 6:00 a.m. and wiping butts. I was committed.

Six years in, I started getting the itch to find a new goal. I wanted more. I wanted to teach at a higher level, and I wanted a schedule that allowed me to have a family. The more I thought about it, the more I knew I could make it happen. I believed in my ability to attain my goal and started making choices to get there. That's self-efficacy.

This was not always the case. When college ended and most of my classmates bought their one-way tickets to the Big Apple, ready to put their newly minted BFA degrees to work, I convinced myself I wasn't ready. I wasn't good enough. I wasn't thin enough. The last point truly outweighed (pun intended) the first two.

During the spring of my senior year, my program did a talent showcase in New York City for casting agents, and as part of our time there we got to sit down and have lunch with one. I don't remember much of what she said, but I do remember that as she talked about booking commercial work, she directed all her attention at the thin girls in my class before turning to me and saying something like, "Well, you know, you're not that commercial."

Now, almost twenty years later, the joke is on her because I have booked many commercials in my career. As it turns out, people who look like normal people sell products. Who knew? But at that time my plus-size twenty-two-year-old self, with too much self-tanner and too little backbone, didn't know any better, so I believed her.

Bandura identified four ways to improve self-efficacy: mastery experiences, vicarious experiences, verbal persuasion, and physiological arousal.[3] Mastery experiences are our wins, when we take on a challenge and succeed.[4] It makes sense that if you prepare for an interview and get the job, your opinion of your interview skills and your belief that you have the ability to interview successfully will both increase.

Vicarious experiences are when we see someone else succeeding and then base our own opinions about our ability to succeed at a similar task on how similar or different we are from that person. Vicarious experiences are every single Instagram ad/story/reel where a fat person shares how they lost weight; where an overworked, unorganized mom gets her life together; and where a poor person becomes rich. They're inspiring. They're motivating. Especially when the person sharing the experience is a lot like you.

Verbal persuasion is exactly what it sounds like: being your own hype woman. It's sitting in your office before the meeting with your boss where you are going to ask for raise and reminding yourself of all the reasons you deserve one. It's preparing to have an important conversation with your partner by telling yourself, out loud, that you are worthy of love and respect and that if the relationship ends you will be okay. Verbal persuasion can also be encouraging words from someone else. When I'm doubting myself or second-guessing my choices, I turn to my best friends, who are always there with a thoughtful meme and a reminder of my greatness.

Psychological arousal recognizes the link between being tired and being able to do your best work. Basically, when you're tired, you're not at your best—and neither is your belief in your own ability. (If you need a refresher on the importance of sleep, refer to chapter 7.)

The General Self-Efficacy Scale

Self-efficacy is commonly measured using the General Self-Efficacy Scale (GSE). The GSE is a ten-item questionnaire designed by Matthias Jerusalem and Ralf Schwarzer in 1981. It's been used by hundreds of thousands of participants and is currently available in thirty-two languages.[5]

To get an idea of your own level of self-efficacy, respond to the following statements with 1—Not true at all, 2—Hardly true, 3—Moderately true, or 4—Exactly true.

1. I can always manage to solve difficult problems if I try hard enough.
2. If someone opposes me, I can find the means and ways to get what I want.
3. It is easy for me to stick to my aims and accomplish my goals.
4. I am confident that I could deal efficiently with unexpected events.
5. Thanks to my resourcefulness, I know how to handle unforeseen situations.
6. I can solve most problems if I invest the necessary effort.
7. I can remain calm when facing difficulties because I can rely on my coping abilities.
8. When I am confronted with a problem, I can usually find several solutions.
9. If I am in trouble, I can usually think of a solution.
10. I can usually handle whatever comes my way.

When you've finished, add up your total, which should range from 10 to 40.

Results

- 30–40: You have a high level of self-efficacy. You believe in your ability to accomplish your goals and that your actions are responsible for your successes. You continue to believe in your abilities, even when things become difficult. You don't back down from a challenge, in fact, you often seek out what is outside your comfort zone because you see each challenge as an opportunity for growth.

- 20–30: Your self-efficacy could use some work. You might shy away from experiences and challenges that threaten your abilities or self-esteem, and it might take you a while to recover from a negative experience or setback. You sometimes lower your aspirations and expectations for yourself because you don't believe in your abilities.
- 10–20: It's time to dig deep. You are experiencing some serious self-doubt, and it's time to turn that ship around. Your low self-efficacy may leave you more susceptible to depression, anxiety, and stress. When challenges arise, you tend to give up, and you often procrastinate when a task is out of your comfort zone.

Skill Up: Increasing Self-Efficacy

If your GSE score is lower than you want it to be, don't worry. Instead, try these ways to increase your self-efficacy, and if you need a little verbal persuasion, look no further. Whatever it is that you're working toward—a new job, starting your own business, giving a fantastic presentation, whatever it is—my wish for you is to recognize that your voice has power and that you have all the tools to use that power to go after it. You can ask for what you want and get it. You can persuade others to your point of view. You can speak and be heard.

Try Something New

Dr. Nicole Celestine, a researcher at the University of Western Australia and writer about all things psychological, recommends pushing yourself to try something new:

- Take a workshop or class in something you're interested in but have never tried.
- Go to a social event and introduce yourself to new people.
- Train for a race or try a new fitness class.
- Take a day trip to somewhere you've never been before.[6]

Celestine says that seizing the opportunity to engage in new, meaningful pursuits gives us the chance to succeed in new ways and develop resilience when we fail. I find that the thrill of succeeding at something new is stronger than succeeding at something I already know how to do.

I am not a runner. I love to dance, I love step aerobics, I love spinning, but running outdoors, in the elements, without an Energizer Bunny–esque instructor constantly reminding me that my brain is stronger than my body and that I didn't come this far to only come this far? No, thank you. Which is why when one of my best girlfriends suggested I come down to visit her in Austin so we could run a half-marathon together, my first reaction was, "I'm sorry, this is Jessica; have we met?"

But thanks to her superhuman powers of verbal persuasion (and a promise that we could spend the rest of the trip at a spa), I agreed. I spent the next six months preparing for the race. It was still winter in Michigan, so at first, I ran on the treadmill at the gym. That wasn't so bad because I could watch both Netflix and the countdown clock to take my mind off the fact that I was actually in motion. As the weather improved and the race date neared, I decided it was time to head outside, and to do that I needed a color-coordinated running wardrobe.

Two days and several hundred dollars later, I stepped onto the sidewalk in front of my apartment building and began my first outdoor run. I had my playlist and my new hydration running belt and shiny water bottle filled with Riptide Rush Gatorade, and I was clad in head-to-toe black Lycra with hot pink accents. I was ready. I did five miles that day and was officially in good enough shape that I was running (or jogging) more than I was walking. The end of that run was the first time I started to feel like a runner—and shockingly, I liked it. I started dropping "I'm a runner" into conversations whenever I had the chance.

The day of the race came, and it didn't matter that I had no chance of winning or that the course was full of hills and I had only trained on flat ground. I loved it. I loved the crowd cheering with their handmade signs. I loved the woman in front of me whose shirt said, "I thought they said 'Rum.'" I loved grabbing the little paper cups of water from the race volunteers, guzzling it, and then tossing the cup on the ground because I could not stop my 5.5 mph pace to throw it in the trash can.

I didn't know it at the time, but I was totally building my self-efficacy. I was believing in my ability to accomplish a new—and really big—goal. And I did it. A win.

Ask for Feedback

In his article for medium.com on increasing self-efficacy, psychologist Larry G. Maguire suggests asking for and accepting feedback. Maguire says that people who have high levels of self-efficacy don't take their failures personally; instead, they attribute failure to a lack of preparedness or skill, something they can then work to overcome.[7] To ask for feedback:

- Ask people you trust, whose feedback will be helpful to you.
- Be specific in your feedback request. Try to stay away from broad questions like, "Did I do a good job?"
- Remind yourself to be open to receiving the information. Feedback is not a slight to you as a human being, but ways in which you can improve a specific set of skills.

Every Friday I teach a studio class for all the musical theatre majors in the program, about fifty students in total. The class is a chance for us all to get together and for me to have face time with the group as a whole, but mostly it's a chance for students to try out pieces they're working on and receive feedback.

Whenever a student gets up to sing, I start by asking them what they'll be singing, if it's for a particular class or audition, and what they'd like feedback on. I instruct them to be specific in their request for feedback: Are they struggling with a particular verse or passage? Is the story they're trying to tell coming across clearly? Are the jokes landing? That way the audience knows what to look and listen for and the student knows what to expect. It also sets up the feedback session as being positive and helpful rather than "Here's what you're doing wrong."

Then I instruct the rest of the students to structure their feedback using what my mother calls "the sandwich approach." The sandwich approach (which could be the title of my mom's autobiography should she ever write one) is positive-negative-positive. You start with a positive comment about the work, which from my students is usually something like, "OMG I'm obsessed with your voice" or the ever-popular "You *slayed.*" Then you talk about what you think needs improvement. Finally, you end with another positive comment.

I love giving my students the opportunity to give feedback, because it means they understand what we've been learning. You can't talk about a concept (at least not well) unless you fully understand it. This is also why it's important to choose the right people to give you feedback. Your grandma might tell you you're amazing, but if you're a finance wizard and she doesn't know anything about developing an investment portfolio, her feedback isn't going to be the most helpful.

Celebrate Success

Another suggestion from Maguire is to celebrate success: your own and that of those around you. We're often so focused on our failures and our "needs improvement" areas that we forget all the things we're doing right.

- At the end of each day, take a few minutes to reflect on what went well. If you're so inclined, write your successes down in a journal so you have them to look at when you're having an off day.

- Be the kind of friend who says good things about others behind their back. Brag about your friends, especially your girlfriends, when they're not around.
- Remember the old adage "If you're the most successful person in the room, you're in the wrong room"? We rise and fall to the level of those around us, so surround yourself with people who motivate you, inspire you, and lift you up.

During the summer of 2021, I had the privilege of being interviewed on the podcast *Embracing Only*, hosted by Archita Fritz and Olivia Cream.[8] As a woman of color working in the field of engineering, Fritz spent most of her professional life as an "only":

> I have felt like "an only" at every step of my life as an adult. First, when I stepped off my plane at age seventeen into the wintry wonderland of the Upper Peninsula of Michigan to pursue my undergraduate studies. I was the only girl in the entire class of men in my computer engineering class. The journey continued into my first internship, where my manager had to hold sensitivity training for his group of engineers because I was the first woman engineer they had hired and the first woman of color engineer in the entire plant.
>
> The list continues between the meeting rooms entered and the spaces shared as I moved through various job opportunities. My "onliness" even extended outside the boardroom, when I decided to marry a man who was not from the community I was raised to believe I would marry into, let alone from India, an "only" experience I continue to embrace as we raise three third-culture kids.

Archita says she didn't always have the examples or the tribe she needed to know that it is possible to thrive in spite of it all, and that lack of support system was her biggest motivator to start the podcast:

> Through the stories of the women we interview, I hope to accomplish two things. One, empower women with actionable ways to focus on the controllables and #killthefear. Two, to empower the women we interview with the power of their own stories. We want to show women that there are many different ways to write your own success story.
>
> I want to leave the women reading this with one of my favorite quotes from Daniele Doby's book *I Am Her Tribe*: "Be around the light bringers, the magic makers, the world shifters, the game shakers. They challenge you, break you open, uplift and expand you. They don't let you play small with your life. These heartbeats are your people. These people are your tribe."[9]

My episode was called "Choose to Challenge with Your Voice." I talked about my work teaching women to harness the power of their voices, to speak up against toxicity, and to ask for what they want. About halfway through the interview, we got on the topic of celebrating success—or rather, how women don't.

Archita told me that at the end of the pandemic, she finally got to have dinner with her close group of girlfriends. Like all of us, they hadn't been in a restaurant, or even in the same room together, for a long time, and she was excited to reconnect. You'd think that after such a dark time, this group of friends would want to celebrate, to express the relief they felt, and to share how good it was to be together. Do you know the first thing they talked about? Their "needs improvement" areas.

They talked about what they were working on: a career shift, fitness goals, relationship changes—which are all important to share and discuss—but what was missing was their wins. It didn't even cross Archita's mind until we were talking about it that this had happened, because it wasn't unusual. I agreed; my girlfriends and I do the exactly the same thing.

Let's normalize celebrating each other. I'll start: The women in my life are smart and funny and strong and beautiful. They're amazing mothers, doctors, nurses, teachers, researchers, and performers. They're my inspiration, my motivation, my shoulder to cry on, and my voice of reason. If your inner circle is anything like mine, they don't just deserve to be celebrated, they deserve a whole damn parade with fire baton twirlers and a marching band playing "Savage Remix" by Megan Thee Stallion and Beyoncé. Okay, now it's your turn.

Be Brave

In her article "Be Brave: How to Build Your Professional Courage," Dr. Tracy Brower breaks courage down into five types: stand with, stand up, stand for, stand down, and still standing:

- Stand with someone in the face of adversity. Stand with them when they've been wronged. Stand with them when they need support.
- Stand up by taking your goals seriously. Stand up for your talents and your greatness. Stand up by holding yourself accountable for your mistakes.
- Stand for by knowing what matters to you and sticking to it. Stand for by making the decision that benefits not only you but those around you as well.
- Stand down by knowing when to pursue and when to compromise. Stand down by taking a step back, allowing time to reassess, and seeing another's point of view.
- Still standing is realizing that courage is a skill that is developed and strengthened over time. Still standing is if

at first you don't succeed, learn from your mistakes, and do better the next time.[10]

SUMMARY

- Accept that if it's important to you, you're going to be nervous. Make your nervous energy work for you by shifting it from "Oh shit, it's almost my turn" into "Let's go! When is it going to be my turn?"
- Walk into the room like you own it. You don't need to be conceited. You don't need to share your inner thoughts with anyone else. You do need to be thinking, "I am the best goddamn X in this room." If you don't believe in your greatness, how is anyone else supposed to?
- Create a ritual. Take a few deep breaths. Stretch down and touch your toes. Spin around three times. Shotgun a beer. Choose a few quick actions that you can do each and every time you speak to center yourself and be in the moment.
- Courage is part nature and part nurture. If you skydive on the weekends while the rest of us are sale hunting at TJ Maxx, it's possible your brain is wired to make you more of a natural risk taker. Even if you're not, courage can be cultivated.
- Self-efficacy is your belief in your own abilities. People with high levels of self-efficacy set big goals because they know that with hard work and determination, they can reach them. People with low self-efficacy often shy away from things outside their comfort zone and take failure personally.
- Albert Bandura, the father of self-efficacy, identified four ways to improve it: mastery experiences, vicarious experiences, verbal persuasion, and psychological arousal. Succeed

at things, be inspired by others like you who succeed at things, be your own hype woman, and get enough sleep.

- Other ways to increase self-efficacy are trying something new, asking for feedback, and celebrating your success and the success of those close to you.
- Dr. Tracy Brower amazingly breaks down courage five ways: stand with, stand up, stand for, stand down, and still standing. Stand with others, stand up for yourself, stand for what matters to you, stand down when it's someone else's turn to take the lead, and remember, when things get rough, why you're still standing.

Chapter 10

The Deep Dive

In the last chapter, I shared with you Dr. Tracy Brower's five types of courage. I was so inspired by her work that I decided to come up with my own. Here are my five tenets of speaking fearlessly: speak with, speak up, speak for, listen, and still speaking.

- **Speak with authenticity.** Speak with a voice that is clear and full of life. Speak with power and poise. Speak with the confidence that your words deserve to be heard.
- **Speak up when you see someone wronged.** Speak up against toxicity in all its forms. Speak up for those who are still too afraid to speak for themselves.
- **Speak for yourself.** Ask for what you want and get what you need.
- **Listen.** Listen to your family, your friends, your colleagues, and your community. Listen to the women in your life, especially women of color. Know when it's time to speak and when it's time to create space so others' voices can be heard.
- **Still speaking.** Skill up on resilience. Skill up on commitment. I often ask my students when they're working on a solo song, "If this was real—if you really were this person,

> and you were really saying these things—why doesn't anyone cut you off?" The answer must be that what you have to say is so important, and you are saying it with such passion and conviction, that you don't give them the chance to. Why don't they cut me off? Because I'm speaking.

This chapter is dedicated to preparing you for specific speaking up situations, both personal and professional. You can read the whole chapter at once or skip around to the parts that relate directly to your needs. Most of the information presented here is taken directly from my workshops.

Be Assertive (without Being a Bitch)

Walking the line between being seen as an assertive leader and being seen as a villain can be tough, especially if you're a firefighter. I don't mean the kind of firefighter with a big red truck, tall ladder, and water hose; I mean someone who, as part of their job, has to put out fires. There's a saying in theatre that if a show goes great, everyone praises the actors, but if it tanks, they blame the director. When you're in charge of anything—a family, a company, a school, a team—it means that more often than not, you're going to deal with the problems more than you're going to celebrate the wins.

In her article for career search website The Muse, social worker and performance coach Melody J. Wilding discusses this topic and gives her advice:

1. To rally the team around your plan—Acknowledge others' ideas. Instead of what I like to call the "because I said so," approach, let your team know that you not only hear their opinions but value them. Also, make sure your ideas stand up under fire. Your team should be able to question your ideas and you should be able to back them up with factual reasoning. For example: "That's a great idea, Alex. How about

we try it for three months instead of six, and then if the numbers don't go the way we want them to, we can adjust."

2. If you ask for a raise and get shut down—Keep your claws in, Wolverine. Remember, you are a professional who respects herself and treats those around her with respect, even when things don't go her way. Instead, try asking your boss for more details about her decision and specific feedback on your performance so you can create tangible goals and targets you both can use when it's time to reevaluate your compensation package down the road.

3. If a member of your team is doing less-than-stellar work—First of all, remember that this is a private, closed-door conversation, not an opportunity to embarrass or degrade anyone as an example for the rest of the team. Next, clearly state how and why his work is falling short, being sure that you are, indeed, talking about the work and not his personal qualities. I like to start conversations like this by reminding myself that everyone is doing the best they can. I have found that for the most part, this holds true. With this in mind, ask him if there is anything else going on that may be negatively affecting his work. If this is out of the ordinary for him, my guess is that there is. Maybe he's going through something in his personal life, or maybe your instructions weren't clear. To help him get things back on track, you schedule a weekly check-in with him and remind him that your door is always open.[1]

Working in higher ed as both a program head and a faculty mentor to students, I deal with the third scenario a lot. Earlier this year, my senior class was going through some growing pains, which is understandable, as they spent almost two of the four years of their college careers in some level of COVID-caused remote instruction. The pandemic created a lot of "new normals";

one of them, for me, was a much laxer approach to attendance and deadlines. When survival becomes an issue, does anything else even matter?

Then we came back. Fall 2022 was my first semester teaching completely "back to normal." No masks, no COVID reports, no quarantine, and no excused absences. And let me tell you, it was a struggle. Missing class, late to class, missing assignments, late assignments, not to mention the students weren't treating each other well. There was an unhealthy competitiveness, and a culture of smiling to someone's face and then ripping them apart behind their back was developing. Three weeks in, I had so many students in my office crying, I was out of tissues—and I was pissed.

What really upset me was that the problem seemed to exist among the women in the senior class, who were tearing each other down. If there's one thing I cannot stand, it's mean girls. My first instinct was to pull the designated perpetrators into my office and ask them what the hell their problem was, throwing in a few choice four-letter words so they knew I was serious. Instead, I took a breath, talked to a few trusted colleagues, and decided to bring the entire senior class together to have a conversation, not a trial.

Two days later, we all sat in a circle, and I started by simply asking the group, "What's going on?" As it turned out, a lot. These young people were hurting. They felt cheated out of two years of their education, which is valid, because in a lot of ways they were. They felt like the opportunities they had left at school were limited, and there was a real fear of missing out on what remained. There was also a lot of personal stuff going on—a whole lot. What it boiled down to was that they were trying to do their best with the hand they had been dealt.

Did that excuse their poor choices? Absolutely not. But coming at the conversation with empathy and respect rather than disappointment and frustration gave me a much clearer understanding of what was fueling the problems and gave them a chance to speak up for themselves and speak with each other. Things aren't perfect now—one conversation can't fix everything—but they're getting better.

Speaking Up against Toxicity

In *Why We Act: Turning Bystanders into Moral Rebels*, author Catherine Sanderson says, "Silence conveys a lack of concern, or even tacit acquiescence. Making it far more likely that it will continue."[2] Seeing toxicity or wrongdoing in any form and choosing to speak up against it not only shows your own courage but also influences others—especially other victims—to speak up too. Activist and survivor Tarana Burke started the #MeToo movement in 2006 and watched as it went viral, almost overnight, in 2017.[3] Why? Because women in the media, led by actress and fellow survivor Alyssa Milano, started speaking up and sharing their stories.[4] Suddenly women from all walks of life were sharing the hashtag and their stories of survival and support.

If you have found yourself wanting to speak up when you witness wrongdoing or stand with someone who has been wronged but have remained silent, forgive yourself. Then commit to putting the skills you've learned in this book to work so that next time you won't stay silent. In the words of the great Maya Angelou, now that you know better, do better.

To prepare, try actively playing out different types of responses to offensive or problematic behavior. The following are from a workshop I was part of for SpeakUp Revolution UK, titled "It's Not You, It's Gaslighting," directed at speaking up against gaslighting. Gaslighting is when you are made to question your own reality, and it can happen personally and professionally.

1. Identify gaslighting. Gaslighting might look like:
    - "You don't know what you're talking about."
    - "You have a bad memory; that's not what happened."

- "This is just another crazy idea you got from your friends."
- "You're being too sensitive/overreacting."
- Telling a woman she is irrational or crazy *because* she is a woman.

2. When you experience or observe gaslighting, stop the behavior and express your concern or disapproval succinctly.[5]
   - "Hey, that's not cool."
   - "No, that's not what happened; don't twist it."
   - "You're telling me X, but I don't see it that way. Can we talk about this?"
3. Assume the comment is sarcastic and identify it as such.[6]
   - "I know you're just trying to be funny, but some people really do think women are too emotional to be leaders."
   - "I know you're being sarcastic, but it could be taken the wrong way."
   - "I don't think everyone appreciates sarcasm; let's refocus."
4. Make the discomfort about you, not them.
   - "That comment is hard for me to hear."
   - "I know you're joking, but that makes me uncomfortable."
   - "You're not hearing me. I'm going to take a break from this conversation, and if you're ready to listen to my point of view, we can pick it back up then."

If you're like me, your first instinct may not be to calmly stop the conversation and politely make the discomfort about you. My first instinct is to let the perpetrator know exactly what I think of their comment and exactly where they can stick it. Particularly if this is a first offense, instead of going immediately on the attack, try to give the other person the benefit of the doubt while still clearly pointing out the problematic behavior. By making your response short and clear, you may be more likely to defuse the situation and move on.

If the behavior is ongoing, involve others who may have also been witness to it and, if need be, involve HR. There is strength in numbers, and having more than one voice backing up a claim may help it be taken more seriously.

How to Communicate Anything Better

This info comes from an interview I did in 2021 with *Real Estate Business* magazine.[7] The article is aimed at helping real estate agents up their presentation and communication skills, but the information is easily transferable to most professional settings.

1. Address your audience's concerns. People want to know what you can do for them and how you can solve the problems they have. How do you know what they want? Ask. A great way to start a presentation or conversation is by asking your audience what matters to them most and/or what their most pressing concerns are.

2. Presenting challenging information? Find the approach that works best for you. "I have good news, and I have bad news. . . ." You might prefer to give the good news first so that when it comes time to talk about the challenge, your audience feels like they can handle whatever comes their way. Or you might work better addressing the problem straight away, then spending the rest of your time finding solutions.

3. Welcome other suggestions that might work. Even if you're a seasoned expert, sometimes your audience may know details about your topic that you don't. Everyone likes to be

heard, and taking valid suggestions not only improves your presentation but also helps you connect with your audience.

Asking for suggestions can also be a great way to throw yourself a lifeline if you get a little out of your depth. In college, I was the TA for a Theatre 1000 class, a large lecture class for non–theatre majors that was a general education credit option. The professor gave weekly lectures and then the two hundred–plus students in the class broke into groups of about twenty-five and were assigned to a TA to work in more detail.

This was my first time teaching in this capacity and I had absolutely no idea what I was doing, including that in order to discuss the plays assigned each week, I also had to read them. The syllabus (which I did not read) clearly stated that in the second week of class, the assigned play was *Agamemnon* (which I did not read). That same week of class also happened to be the week the professor decided to pop in and see how I was doing. Shit.

What did I do? Well, I'd spent almost four years studying an art form that requires you to think on your feet, so I improvised. I asked for suggestions: "What was the play about?" "What was the climax?" "Tell me about the protagonist." If I was asked a question directly, I deflected: "Great question! Does anyone have an answer for that?" I finished the class, and the professor told me I was off to a great start. And they say you don't use the skills you learn in college.

Having the Hard Conversations

Having a difficult or emotional conversation is often far more about listening and reflecting on what the other person is saying than it is about your own words. This was a tough lesson for me, as coming up with responses to imaginary conversations is one of my favorite pastimes. Nine-year-old Jessica spent many an afternoon standing in front of the bathroom mirror practicing both her "movie star smile" and what she would say to her fourth grade frenemy Nichole if only she had the chance. (Side note: Nichole and I are now friends. She's an advertising and marketing wiz who owns her own agency, Red Fish Viral, and she was kind enough to take the time out of her busy schedule to speak with me about publishing when I was first exploring what it might look like to write this book. She's a gem.)

The problem with imaginary conversations, other than that they're a complete waste of time and energy, is that they're almost always vastly different than the actual conversation. I can attest to this because for the first few years of my marriage, whenever I needed to have an important conversation with my husband, I would spend at least a week preparing what I was going to say *and* what I was sure his response would be. When we actually had the conversation and he inevitably did not respond how I assumed he would, my response was often . . . less than optimal.

Instead of spending time ruminating over how you imagine a difficult conversation is going to go, try these tips from executive leadership coach Joel Garfinkle:

- Pay attention. People are more likely to share and elaborate on their feelings when they feel like their words matter.
- Ask lots of questions, but try to reserve judgment.
- Be direct and don't postpone the conversation. In the words of the queen Brené Brown, "Clear is kind; unclear is unkind."[8]
- Remember: All's well that ends well. Going into the conversation expecting it to go well makes you more likely to have that conversation and to be less hesitant about future conversations.[9]

Dealing with the "No"

Rejection sucks. I'm not going to elaborate on this point because if you're a human being over the age of knowing what "no" means, you've experienced it, probably more than a few times. What I am going to talk about is how to deal with hearing "no." My personal approach involves drinking several glasses of Juan Gil Spanish red wine and crying in the shower, often at the same time. If you're looking for an approach that does absolutely nothing to bolster resilience but sure feels good, I highly recommend this one. If you're looking for something a little, shall we say, deeper, consider these:

1. Manage your expectations. It has been said that "expectation is the root of all heartache." By all means, have big dreams and make big plans, but also realize that plans take time to accomplish. Most success stories are chock-full of failure. Few people get it right the first time. Remind yourself that "no" right now doesn't mean "no" forever.[10]

2. Don't wallow. You are allowed to be sad. You are allowed to be upset. When disappointment happens, you are allowed to feel all your feelings. Don't let those feelings drag you down across the depression bridge and into the land of apathy. Give yourself all the time you need to feel whatever way you do, and then move on.

3. Remember why you started. Remembering your "why" is one of those super popular phrases used by everyone from self-help gurus to fitness instructors to the pharaoh at the top of an MLM pyramid. There are days I hear it and have to try really hard not to throw up in my mouth. However, when you've been at something for a while and it's not going as far or as fast as you want it to, try reminding yourself why you started in the first place.

VOCAL HEALTH CONCERNS

Here are a few specific vocal health concerns not covered in the rest of the book. This information should never take the place of a medical evaluation but may be helpful in determining if it's time to see a physician or speech language pathologist.

Frequent Throat Clearing or Constantly Having a Lump in Your Throat

Globus pharyngeus, the medical term for feeling like you constantly have a lump in your throat, is one of the most common symptoms of laryngeal pharyngeal reflux (LPR).[11] You are probably familiar with gastroesophageal reflux (GERD), the backing up of stomach acid into the esophagus associated with heartburn, but you may not be as familiar with this second type of reflux. LPR, the backing up of stomach acid into the larynx or voice box, has been referred to as "silent reflux" because it doesn't cause symptoms in the chest.[12] Along with throat clearing, persistent cough, and hoarseness, most people suffering from LPR experience globus pharyngeus.[13]

If you experience these symptoms, take a look at your diet. A diet full of acidic foods such as pasta sauce, fried foods, citrus fruits, chocolate, cheese, and garlic (or, as I tell my students, all that is good in life) is a known contributor to LPR.[14] Along with watching your diet choices, get in the habit of making your larger meals earlier in the day and not eating within three hours before going to bed. More food in the stomach equals more acid being used to digest it, and lying down shortly after eating a large meal makes it more likely that acid will back up into the throat.

Here are some ways to reduce the symptoms associated with LPR:

- Sleep on an angle, either by propping yourself up on pillows or propping up the head of your bed.
- Avoid wearing tight clothing, especially around your midsection.

- Limit your intake of acidic beverages: coffee, caffeinated tea, soda pop, and alcohol.
- Don't smoke or frequent smoke-filled places.
- Limit the use of aspirin and ibuprofen.
- Try to limit throat clearing by coughing purposefully or swallowing. Persistent throat clearing can irritate the vocal folds causing them to swell.

In addition to lifestyle changes, it may be necessary to control LPR with medication such as a proton pump inhibitor, histamine blocker, or antacid. To find out more about these and determine if they're right for you, consult your doctor.

Use of NSAIDs

Nonsteroidal anti-inflammatory drugs (NSAIDs) are a family of over-the-counter drugs commonly used to treat fever and pain, including ibuprofen (Advil, Motrin) and naproxen (Aleve). The problem with NSAID use is that in addition to relieving pain, they are also blood thinners. The vocal folds are full of blood vessels, and those blood vessels can burst due to trauma. When you're under the weather, heavy coughing and frequent throat clearing are par for the course; they're also two of the main causes of trauma that may lead to vocal fold hemorrhage.

A vocal fold hemorrhage is similar to a bruise. The blood pools, and over time, the body will reabsorb it. While the hemorrhage is present, the speaker may experience mild to severe hoarseness, a flutter in the voice, neck pain, and an acute loss of all or part of the vocal range.[15] When the blood is thinner due to the use of NSAIDS, the bruise gets larger, creates more issues for the speaker, and takes longer to heal.

In order for a vocal hemorrhage to heal, the vocal folds need to rest, meaning you have to be quiet. This is a tall order for many women I know, both because they like to talk and because they need to talk. To reduce the likelihood of a vocal hemorrhage, watch misuse and overuse of the voice: yelling, shouting, talking loudly for an extended period of time, frequent throat clearing, and frequent coughing. In addition, if you're under the weather and know you'll be using your voice, or you want to reduce suspected vocal fold swelling, stick to acetaminophen (Tylenol).

Use of Antihistamines and Decongestants

When you have a cold, upper respiratory infection, or seasonal allergies, a common solution to the never-ending snot and phlegm is the use of drying medications such as antihistamines and decongestants. While antihistamines (Benadryl, Allegra, Zyrtec) and decongestants (Sudafed, DayQuil) do a great job of drying up mucus, they don't differentiate between good mucus and bad mucus, which means they dry up your vocal fold tissues right along with your nasal passages.

When the vocal folds are dehydrated, they have to work harder to create sound. In addition, when the tissues of the vocal tract are dry, it often results in the constant need to cough, which can cause the folds to swell.[16]

I'm not saying you shouldn't use these medications. There have been many days I've gone to work living on DayQuil and a prayer. But when you need to use them, be sure you also increase your hydration: Drink more water and try using a saline nasal spray, humidifier, and/or personal steamer.

Other Drugs

Both over-the-counter and prescription medications may affect the voice and speech. If you're interested in the effect your medications may be having on your voice, check in with your doctor. You can also visit the National Center for Voice and Speech website, which lists many medications, including biologics, and the effects they have on voice and speech.[17]

What to Do When You're Sick

Getting a cold or upper respiratory infection can wreak havoc on your voice. Increased mucus production, reduced lung capacity, swollen vocal folds, muscle aches, and fatigue make speaking difficult, especially giving a talk or presentation. If you find yourself under the weather and required to use your voice, try these suggestions to get through your event as easily and healthfully as possible:

- Reduce voice use. You don't need to stop using your voice completely (unless you have laryngitis), but you do need to be mindful of how much and to what extent you're using it. If you have an event that is going to be vocally taxing, reduce voice use during the rest of the day to compensate.
- Take vocal naps. A good rule of thumb when you're under the weather is that if you don't need to be talking, don't talk. Take the opportunity to rest your voice throughout the day.
- Take the medicine. There is no need to suffer needlessly; in fact, not taking cough medicine and spending the day hacking and banging your vocal folds together could be more harmful than the drying effects of the medicine itself.
- Hydrate. Again, if you're taking an antihistamine or decongestant, increase your water intake. A speech language pathologist friend of mine swears by using a $2 bottle of sprayable saline when she's sick to keep her nasal passages lubricated and the extra mucus thin and able to be easily removed.
- Try a tea or lozenge with slippery elm. The mucilage in slippery elm, which combined with moisture creates a gel-like coating, has been scientifically proven to create a feeling of lubrication in the mouth and throat.[18]

- Gargle with salt water. This may not provide immediate pain relief from a sore throat, but it has been proven to soothe inflamed tissues, kill bacteria, and loosen troublesome mucus.[19]

Some Final Thoughts

Being able to speak freely is a right denied to so many women in our world today—too many women. Even in countries where women are free to speak, so many don't because no one ever taught them how. I'm a firm believer that when you know better, you can do better. That belief is what fuels my work and my writing. I hope you take the skills you learned in this book and use them to their fullest extent. I hope the information in this book lights a fire in you to not only imagine what is possible but to go after it, to speak it into existence. Your voice is powerful, and in the way you speak to others and the way you speak to yourself lies the power to change your entire life and the lives of those in your family, your community, your country, and the world. My wish is that you master the skills in this book so you can pass them on.

If you were raised without a strong female role model, if you were raised in a family where women didn't speak up, if you were raised in a family where women spoke up but weren't heard: I hope you will take the skills you learned in this book and put them to use, not only to change your life, but to change the lives of the girls and women around you. I hope you realize that by using your voice, you are becoming a role model for the next generation. You are helping to create a world where seeing a woman speak up isn't special, it's commonplace.

If you have dreams but don't believe they can ever come true, if you have goals but lack the guidance or resources to go after them: I hope you will take the skills you learned in this book and put them to use by talking to those who are where you want to be about how they got there. I hope you will use your newfound voice to ask for what you want and make damn sure you get what you need. And once you do, share it.

I hope you will realize that your voice is not only powerful but also precious, and I hope you realize this *before* you need it and it's not there. Your voice is the one thing that no one else has or will ever have. It can't be donated. It can't be given away. And it can't be taken from you. So treat it well. Treat your voice, your body, and your mind like they are rare, endangered, priceless commodities, because they are. Prioritize your sleep. Drink enough water. Eat nutritious food. Take a steamy shower. Do some humming through a straw. Rest. Laugh. Sing. Breathe. Share. Support. Use your voice, your body, and your mind to their full potential—because when you do, your power is limitless.

Summary

- When speaking assertively, acknowledge others' ideas and back up your own with facts rather than emotions. If you don't get the answer you were hoping for, ask for feedback rather than going on the defensive. When having a conversation that includes performance critique, do it privately, ask questions, and assume everyone is doing their best.
- When speaking up against toxic behavior, do so right away and be direct. Rather than putting the other person on the defensive, assume their comment was sarcastic and identify it as such, let them know that you're uncomfortable, or walk away from the conversation, offering to return once you can be heard.
- When presenting or pitching, know your audience, speak to their top concerns, and offer actionable solutions. Find your own preferred way of presenting tough information: the good news first to soften the blow or the bad news first to rally the troops. Welcome suggestions from your

audience; even if you're an expert, they may present ideas you hadn't previously considered.

- Having a difficult conversation is often more about listening than speaking. Pay attention to what the other person is saying, ask questions without judgment, be direct, and expect the talk to go well. Expecting a positive outcome may make you less likely to postpone having the conversation.
- Deal with disappointment by allowing yourself to feel sad, but don't wallow. Reflect on your own expectations and whether they were realistic, and remember why you started in the first place.
- Hoarseness, coughing, frequent throat clearing, and the feeling of constantly having a lump in your throat are all common symptoms of laryngopharyngeal reflux. Reducing LPR symptoms may require both behavior modifications and medicine.
- Be careful of using NSAIDs when you're under the weather. In addition to relieving pain and fever, they thin the blood, which may increase the severity of a vocal hemorrhage.
- When you're ill, reduce voice use, take vocal naps, increase hydration, and prioritize rest. You can also use a tea or lozenge with slippery elm, which provides a gel-like coating to the mouth and throat.
- Speak with authenticity. Speak up when you see someone wronged. Speak for yourself. Listen. Skill up on resilience and keep speaking.

Acknowledgments

This book would not have been possible without the help of the following people who gave me the gifts of their time, their talents, and their unwavering support.

To my husband, Don, thank you for believing in me and this book, even when I didn't. Thank you for giving me the gift of time to focus and write. Thank you for being my biggest cheerleader, my sounding board, and my safe place. I love you, always.

To my dad, Terry Doyle, who gave teenage me the complete works of William Shakespeare with a note: "If you want to be a great writer, you have to read the great writers." This book is the start of my complete works. Thank you for letting me constantly tap into your wealth of knowledge on the brain and how we learn. Your work is essential to this book, and I am so grateful for it and for you. I love you.

To my mom, Julie Doyle, my best friend and role model for balancing this crazy life of work and family. Growing up with a strong female role model who wasn't afraid to use her voice was essential not only to this book but to making me who I am today. I love you.

To my brother, Brendan Doyle, you are brilliant and destined for great things. Thank you for being the next generation of Doyles studying and writing about learning. Your work is essential. I love you.

To my in-laws, Don and Shannon Mekkes, thank you for making me your own and for loving me relentlessly. Don, thank you for always being so interested in my work and sharing all my posts on LinkedIn. Your support means so much to me. Shan, thank you for caring for me and my family so completely. To be loved by you is to know someone is always in your corner, and that is such a blessing. I love you both.

To my amazing agent, Katharine Sands, thank you for taking a chance on a new writer and for believing in this book from day one. Thank you for offering such valuable feedback during the shaping (and reshaping) of the proposal. Thank you for the time and effort you spent finding a home for my book. I am an author because of you. Thank you, thank you, thank you.

To Jessica Sinsheimer, thank you recommending me to Katharine. You didn't need to take the time, but you did. For that, I am forever grateful.

To my editor, Suzanne Staszak-Silva, Mary Wheelehan, Joanna Wattenberg, and the entire team at Rowman & Littlefield, thank you for making this dream of mine a reality. I am forever grateful for the opportunity and for all your guidance and care. Thank you.

To my inner circle—Alexa, Emily, Jillian, Katie, and Modie—thank you for being the voices in my head. Thank you for your love, care, friendship, and trust. Thank you for making me laugh and being there when I cry. Thank you for being strong women and raising strong women. Reva, Ellida, Chloe, Quinn, and Modestina are going to take over the world. Thank you also for being my first readers and for your thoughtful comments. I love you all.

To my dear friend Bryan Conger, whose words appear throughout this book: I wouldn't get through the workday without you. I'm so grateful you came into my life and into my family's lives. I love you.

To my dear friend Jessica Teague, thank you for lending me your tigers. You are such a light in my life, and I am so grateful for you. I love you.

To my friends and colleagues at the ECU School of Theatre and Dance, thank you for your support and for making going to work each day something I look forward to. Few people are lucky enough to spend their days doing what they love among people they genuinely enjoy, and I get to do both. Thank you.

To Tracy Watson, Meghan Dewald-Althouse, and Latoya Lain-Washington, thank you for accepting me into the MM program at CMU, even though I only knew three classical songs. Your guidance, mentorship, and friendship are such a gift, especially as we all navigate this thing called working motherhood as artists. Thank you.

To Jeffrey Foote, thank you for teaching me how to drop my jaw and sing like a champion.

To Alan Gumm, thank you for helping me fall in love with research. The work in this book would not have been possible without the skills you taught me.

To Archita Fritz and Alexandra Knight, thank you for taking the time to share your stories. Your work is inspiring and empowering women—including me—every day. You are superheroes.

To Frances Holmes and Marie Hemmingway at SpeakOut Revolution, thank you for including me and my work in your crusade to make the workplace and the world a safer space for all women.

To the amazing professionals who gave of their time to support this book long before it was a book—Amanda Smith, George Aquino, Maria Dalisay, Emily Comerford, Susan Michelson, and Jes Van—thank you for your time and your support. I am forever grateful.

To the extraordinary women of Momology 4, Peloton Moms, and the Peloton Book Club who helped with the title of this book, thank you. I can't wait for you to read it.

To my students, thank you for (usually) showing up and working so hard. ;) You teach me as much as I teach you. Go change the world.

Notes

Introduction

1. Georgene Huang, "What Has Changed in the Workplace for Women a Year after #MeToo," *Forbes*, October 30, 2018. https://www.forbes.com/sites/georgenehuang/2018/10/30/what-has-changed-in-the-workplace-for-women-a-year-after-metoo/.

2. "New Research Reveals Different Perspectives on Workplace Culture," *Los Angeles Business Journal*, June 29, 2021, https://labusinessjournal.com/news/2021/jun/29/new-research-reveals-differences-perspectives-work/.

3. Jennifer Ludden, "Ask for a Raise? Most Women Hesitate," *All Things Considered*, February 8, 2011, https://www.npr.org/2011/02/14/133599768/ask-for-a-raise-most-women-hesitate.

4. Megan Leonhardt, "60% of Women Say They've Never Negotiated Their Salary and Many Quit Their Job Instead," CNBC, January 31, 2020, https://www.cnbc.com/2020/01/31/women-more-likely-to-change-jobs-to-get-pay-increase.html.

5. Kristin Blakemore Edwards, "Even Powerful Women Struggle to Speak Up in a Meeting Full of Men: Here's How to Change That," *Inc.*, July 21, 2017, https://www.inc.com/partners-in-leadership/breaking-the-silence-in-the-boardroom-even-when-yo.html.

Chapter 1: Meet Your Voice

1. Susan McPherson, "Meet the Winner of the DVF Awards' 2016 People's Voice Award," *Forbes*, May 10, 2016. https://www.forbes.com/sites/susanmcpherson/2016/05/10/meet-the-winner-of-the-dvf-awards-2016-peoples-choice-award/.

2. Stacey Ramsower, "The Vocal-Vaginal Correlation," *Baby Chick* (blog), August 10, 2021, https://www.baby-chick.com/vocal-vaginal-correlation/.

3. Ramsower, "The Vocal-Vaginal Correlation."

4. Wendy DeLeo LeBorgne and Marci Daniels Rosenberg, "Role of the Larynx," in *The Vocal Athlete: Application and Technique for the Hybrid Singer* (San Diego, CA: Plural Publishing, 2021), 47.

5. LeBorgne and Rosenberg, "Role of the Larynx," 47.

6. Neil Bhattacharyya, "The Prevalence of Voice Problems among Adults in the United States," *Laryngoscope* 124, no. 10 (October 2014): 2359–62, https://doi.org/10.1002/lary.24740.

7. American Speech-Language-Hearing Association, "Voice Disorders," https://www.asha.org/practice-portal/clinical-topics/voice-disorders/.

8. Regina Helena Garcia Martins, Eny Regina Bóla Neves Pereira, Calo Bosque Hidalgo, and Elaine Lara Mendes Tavares, "Voice Disorders in Teachers. A Review," *Journal of Voice* 28, no. 6 (June 2014), http://doi.org/10.1016/j.jvoice.2014.02.008.

9. American Speech-Language-Hearing Association, "Voice Disorders."

10. Mayo Clinic, "Aerobic Exercise: How to Warm Up and Cool Down," https://www.mayoclinic.org/healthy-lifestyle/fitness/in-depth/exercise/art-20045517.

11. Voice Science Works, "SOVT Exercises," https://www.voicescienceworks.org/sovt-exercises.html.

12. LeBorgne and Rosenberg, "Role of the Larynx," 60–65.

13. Leslie Childs, "Voice Care: Sorting Fact from Fiction," *MedBlog*, April 13, 2020, https://utswmed.org/medblog/vocal-cords-care-qa/.

14. Mahalakshmi Sivasankar and Ciara Leydon, "The Role of Hydration in Vocal Fold Physiology," *Current Opinion in Otolaryngology and Head and Neck Surgery* 18, no. 3 (June 2010): 171–75, https://doi.org/10.1097%2FMOO.0b013e3283393784.

15. Gemma Saunders, "How to Take Care of Your Vocal Cords for Singing: Voice Care for Singers," *Open Mic UK*, updated November 13, 2019, https://www.openmicuk.co.uk/advice/how-to-take-care-of-your-voice-and-vocal-cords/.

16. Michael Breus, "The Relationship between Water and Sleep Health and How to Avoid Dehydration," *The Sleep Doctor* (blog), September 9, 2022, https://www.bipmd.com/news/the-relationship-between-water-and-sleep-health-how-to-avoid-dehydration.

17. Sivasankar and Leydon, "The Role of Hydration in Vocal Fold Physiology."

18. Sophie C. Killer, Andrew K. Blannin, and Asker E. Jeukendrup, "No Evidence of Dehydration with Moderate Daily Coffee Intake: A Counterbalanced Cross-over Study in a Free-Living Population," *PLOS ONE* 9, no. 1 (2014): e84154, https://doi.org/10.1371/journal.pone.0084154.

19. Wendy DeLeo LeBorgne and Marci Daniels Rosenberg, "Medicine Myths & Truths," in *The Vocal Athlete*, 565–66.

20. LeBorgne and Rosenberg, "Medicine Myths & Truths," 565–66.

21. Shenbagavalli Mahalingam and Prakash Boominathan, "Effects of Steam Inhalation on Voice Quality–Related Acoustic Measures," *Laryngoscope* 126, no. 10 (October 2016): 2305–2309, https://doi.org/10.1002/lary.25933.

22. Wendy DeLeo LeBorgne and Marci Daniels Rosenberg, "Exercise Physiology Principles for Training the Vocal Athlete," in *The Vocal Athlete*, 320.

23. Katherine R. Arlinghaus and Craig A. Johnston, "The Importance of Creating Habits and Routine," *American Journal of Lifestyle Medicine* 13, no. 2 (March–April 2019): 142–44, https://doi.org/10.1177%2F1559827618818044.

24. Lee Akst, "Phonotrauma," Johns Hopkins Medicine, https://www.hopkinsmedicine.org/health/conditions-and-diseases/phonotrauma.

25. Akst, "Phonotrauma."

26. Wendy DeLeo LeBorgne and Marci Daniels Rosenberg, "Common Vocal Pathologies," in *The Vocal Athlete*, 155–57.

27. American Speech-Language-Hearing Association, "Vocal Cord Nodules and Polyps," https://www.asha.org/public/speech/disorders/vocal-cord-nodules-and-polyps/.

28. National Institute on Deafness and Other Communication Disorders, "Taking Care of Your Voice," https://www.nidcd.nih.gov/health/taking-care-your-voice.

29. Eric J. Hunter, Kristine Tanner, and Marshall E. Smith, "Gender Differences Affecting Vocal Health of Women in Vocally Demanding Careers," *Logopedics Phoniatrics Vocology* 36, no. 3 (October 2011): 128–36, https://doi.org/10.3109%2F14015439.2011.587447.

30. Ofer Amir and Tal Biron-Shental, "The Impact of Hormonal Fluctuations on Female Vocal Folds," *Current Opinion in Otolaryngology and Head and Neck Surgery* 12, no. 3 (June 2004): 180–84, https://doi.org/10.1097/01.moo.0000120304.58882.94.

31. Jean Abitbol, Patric Abitbol, and Béatrice Abitbol, "Sex Hormones and the Female Voice," *Journal of Voice* 13, no. 3 (September 1999): 424–46, https://doi.org/10.1016/S0892-1997(99)80048-4.

32. Kay Wilhelm, Gordon Parker, Liesbeth Geerligs, and Lucinda Wedgwood, "Women and Depression: A 30 Year Learning Curve," *Australian and New Zealand Journal of Psychiatry* 42, no. 1 (January 2008): 3–12, https://doi.org/10.1080/00048670701732665; Hunter, Tanner, and Smith, "Gender Differences Affecting Vocal Health of Women in Vocally Demanding Careers"; Dolores Jurado, Manuel Gurpegui, Obdulia Moreno, M. Carmen Fernández, Juan D. Luna, and Ramón Galvez, "Association of Personality and Work Conditions with Depressive Symptoms," *European Psychiatry* 20, no. 3 (May 2005): 213–22, https://doi.org/10.1016/j.eurpsy.2004.12.009; Maria Dietrich, Katherine Verdolini Abbott, Jackie Gartner-Schmidt, and Clark A. Rosen, "The Frequency of Perceived Stress, Anxiety, and Depression in Patients with Common Pathologies Affecting Voice," *Journal of Voice* 22, no. 4 (July 2008): 472–88, https://doi.org/10.1016/j.jvoice.2006.08.007.

33. Tsu-Yu Hsiao, C. M. Liu, C. J. Hsu, S. Y. Lee, and K. N. Lin, "Vocal Fold Abnormalities in Laryngeal Tension-Fatigue Syndrome," *Journal of the Formosan Medical Association* 100, no. 12 (December 2001): 837–40, https://pubmed.ncbi.nlm.nih.gov/11802526/.

34. Vaninder Kaur Dhillon, "Muscle Tension Dysphonia," Johns Hopkins Medicine, https://www.hopkinsmedicine.org/health/conditions-and-diseases/muscle-tension-dysphonia.

35. Dhillon, "Muscle Tension Dysphonia."

36. Hunter, Tanner, and Smith, "Gender Differences Affecting Vocal Health of Women in Vocally Demanding Careers"; Kenneth J. Ellis, "Human Body Composition: In Vivo Methods," *Physiological Reviews* 80, no. 2 (April 2000): 649–80, https://doi.org/10.1152/physrev.2000.80.2.649.

37. Chloe Burcham, "13 Celebrities Speak Honestly about Living with PCOS," *Women's Health*, November 12, 2021, https://www.womenshealthmag.com/uk/health/a38171906/celebrities-with-pcos/.

38. Joelle Goldstein, "Amanda Gorman Tells Oprah Winfrey Why Her Speech Impediment Is 'One of My Greatest Strengths,'" *People*, March 25, 2021, https://people.com/human-interest/amanda-gorman-opens-up-speech-impediment-oprah-winfrey-interview/.

39. Joi-Marie McKenzie, "Oprah Winfrey Opens Up about Her Battle with Depression: 'I Was behind a Veil,'" ABC News, August 14, 2017, https://abcnews.go.com/Entertainment/oprah-winfrey-opens-battle-depression-veil/story?id=49206090.

Chapter 2: Just Breathe

1. Jared Morine, "How Breathing Can Improve Your Voice," *Speech and Voice Global Enterprises*, January 21, 2020, https://speechandvoice.com/blog/1433/How-Breathing-Can-Improve-Your-Voice.

2. James Nestor, *Breath: The New Science of a Lost Art* (London: Penguin Life, 2021), 289–90.

3. Cleveland Clinic, "Parasympathetic Nervous System (PSNS): What It Is & Function," https://my.clevelandclinic.org/health/body/23266-parasympathetic-nervous-system-psn.

4. Cleveland Clinic, "Sympathetic Nervous System (SNS): What It Is & Function," https://my.clevelandclinic.org/health/body/23262-sympathetic-nervous-system-sns-fight-or-flight.

5. Nestor, *Breath*, 289–90.

6. Nestor, *Breath*, 289–90.

7. Nestor, *Breath*, 292.

8. Jeri Innis, "Anxious or Worried Sick? What's Autonomic Nervous System Dysregulation?" *Innis Integrative BodyMind Therapy*, November 22, 2016, https://www.innisintegrativetherapy.com/blog/2016/11/22/anxious-or-worried-sick-whats-autonomic-nervous-system-dysregulation.

9. Morton E. Tavel, "Hyperventilation Syndrome: A Diagnosis Usually Unrecognized," *Journal of Internal Medicine and Primary Healthcare* 1 (2017), http://doi.org/10.24966/IMPH-2493/100006.

10. Rosalba Courtney and Jan Van Dixhoorn, "Questionnaires and Manual Methods for Assessing Breathing Dysfunction," in *Recognizing and Treating Breathing Disorders*, 2nd ed., edited by Leon Chaitow, Dinah Bradley, and Christopher Gilbert, 137–46 (London: Churchill Livingstone, 2014), https://doi.org/10.1016/B978-0-7020-4980-4.00012-5.

11. Jill Ehrmantraut, "Is Your Breathing Pattern Causing Pelvic Floor Issues?" Apex Physical Therapy and Wellness, https://apexptwellness.com/breath-and-your-pelvic-floor/.

12. Ehrmantraut, "Is Your Breathing Pattern Causing Pelvic Floor Issues?"

13. Emma Ferris, "Posture and Breathing: The Physiological Effects of Shallow Breaths," *The Breath Effect* (blog), December 28, 2018, https://www.thebreatheffect.com/posture-breathing-physiological-effects/.

14. Stevie Rowley, "The History of Shapewear," *L'Officiel*, August 10, 2022, https://www.lofficielusa.com/fashion/the-history-of-shapewear-spanx-skims-corsets-lingere.

15. Rachel Grumman Bender, "Here's What Too-Tight Shapewear Can Actually Do to Your Body," *Self*, March 8, 2017, https://www.self.com/story/what-too-tight-shapewear-can-do-to-your-body.

16. The Chicks, "Wide Open Spaces," track 1 on *Wide Open Spaces*, SBME Special Mkts, 2012.

Chapter 3: The Power of Posture

1. Amy Cuddy, "Your Body Language May Shape Who You Are," TEDGlobal 2012, https://www.ted.com/talks/amy_cuddy_your_body_language_may_shape_who_you_are.

2. David Biello, "Inside the Debate about Power Posing: A Q&A with Amy Cuddy," TED, February 23, 2017, https://ideas.ted.com/inside-the-debate-about-power-posing-a-q-a-with-amy-cuddy/.

3. Wendy DeLeo LeBorgne and Marci Daniels Rosenberg, "Skeletal Structure," in *The Vocal Athlete: Application and Technique for the Hybrid Singer* (San Diego, CA: Plural Publishing, 2021), 51–52.

4. Melinda Malde, MaryJean Allen, and Kurt Alexander Zeller, *What Every Singer Needs to Know about the Body* (San Diego, CA: Plural Publishing, 2009), 61.

5. Coyle Institute, "Your Posture and Your Pelvic Health," https://coyleinstitute.com/your-posture-and-your-pelvic-health/.

6. The FootLab, "Knee, Hip & Back Pain: How Foot Posture Affects Our Joints," https://www.thefootlab.com/knee-hip-back-pain-othotics/.

7. Joanna Shuman, "Time to Take a Heel Break?" Shuman Podiatry, July 17, 2018, https://shumanpodiatry.com/time-to-take-a-heel-break/.

8. Thomas Myers, "Tensegrity," Anatomy Trains, https://www.anatomytrains.com/fascia/tensegrity/.

9. Lukas D. Lopez, Peter J. Reschke, Jennifer M. Knothe, and Eric A. Walle, "Postural Communication of Emotion: Perception of Distinct Poses of Five Discrete Emotions," *Frontiers in Psychology* 8 (May 2017): 710, https://doi.org/10.3389%2Ffpsyg.2017.00710.

10. Hillel Aviezer, Yaacov Trope, and Alexander Todorov, "Body Cues, Not Facial Expressions, Discriminate between Intense Positive and Negative Emotions," *Science* 388, no. 6111 (November 30, 2022), https://doi.org/10.1126/science.1224313; Lisa Feldman Barett, Batja Mesquita, and Maria Gendron, "Context in Emotion Perception," *Current Directions in Psychological Science* 20, no. 5 (2011), https://doi.org/10.1177/0963721411422522; Ran R. Hassin, Hillel Aviezer, and Shlomo Bentin, "Inherently Ambiguous: Facial Expressions of Emotions, in Context," *Emotion Review* 5, no. 1 (January 2013): 60–65, https://doi.org/10.1177/1754073912451331.

11. Ohio State University, "Body Posture Affects Confidence in Your Own Thoughts, Study Finds," *ScienceDaily*, October 5, 2009, https://www.sciencedaily.com/releases/2009/10/091005111627.htm.

Chapter 4: The Nitty Gritty

1. Amy Borel, "What Is Bone Conduction and How Does It Help Us Perceive Sound?" *Forbrain* (blog), June 24, 2021, https://blog.forbrain.com/blog/what-is-bone-conduction-and-how-does-it-help-us-perceive-sound-0.

2. Louisa May Alcott, *Little Women* (Baltimore: Penguin, 1953), 458, https://www.scribd.com/read/367159751/Little-Women.

3. Frances Hodgson Burnett, *The Secret Garden* (New York: F. A. Stokes, NY, 1911), https://www.scribd.com/read/479218534/The-Secret-Garden.

4. George Bernard Shaw, *Pygmalion* (Mineola, NY: Dover, 1994).

5. Jessica Bennett, "What Do We Hear When Women Speak?" *New York Times*, November 20, 2019, https://www.nytimes.com/2019/11/20/us/politics/women-voices-authority.html.

6. James Allen, "Gender Bias in Lecture Acoustics," *What I've Learned as a Hospital Medical Director* (blog), November 29, 2019, https://hospitalmedicaldirector.com/gender-bias-in-lecture-acoustics/.

7. Tina Tallon, "A Century of 'Shrill': How Bias in Technology Has Hurt Women's Voices," *New Yorker*, September 3, 2019, https://www.newyorker.com/culture/cultural-comment/a-century-of-shrill-how-bias-in-technology-has-hurt-womens-voices.

8. Tallon, "A Century of 'Shrill.'"

9. Audrey Hepburn, quoted on Goodreads, https://www.goodreads.com/quotes/241284-i-believe-in-being-strong-when-everything-seems-to-be.

10. Heidi Markham, "You Asked: What Is Vocal Fry?" *Time*, November 2, 2017, https://time.com/5006345/what-is-vocal-fry/.

11. Marissa Fessenden, "Vocal Fry Creeping into US Speech," *Science*, December 9, 2011, https://www.science.org/content/article/vocal-fry-creeping-us-speech.

12. Markham, "You Asked: What Is Vocal Fry?"

13. Rindy C. Anderson, Casey A. Klofstad, William J. Mayew, and Mohan Venkatachalam, "Vocal Fry May Undermine the Success of Young Women in the Labor Market." *PLOS ONE* 9, no. 5 (2014): e97506, https://doi.org/10.1371/journal.pone.0097506.

14. Lottie Winter, "Every Single One of Kim Kardashian West's Businesses—from Dash to Skims—Ranked," *Glamour UK*, September 13, 2022, https://www.glamourmagazine.co.uk/gallery/kim-kardashian-businesses.

15. "Kim Kardashian Passes California 'Baby Bar' Law Exam," BBC News, December 13, 2021, https://www.bbc.com/news/entertainment-arts-59642262.

16. Samantha Rosie, "Top 10 Celebrities Known for Their Frequent Use of Vocal Fry," Top Tens, https://www.thetoptens.com/people/people-celebrities-who-use-vocal-fry/.

17. Monika Chao and Julia R. S. Bursten, "Girl Talk: Understanding Negative Reactions to Female Vocal Fry," *Hypatia* 36, no. 1 (2021): 42–59, https://doi.org/10.1017/hyp.2020.55.

18. Chao and Bursten, "Girl Talk."

19. Chao and Bursten, "Girl Talk."

20. Anderson et al., "Vocal Fry May Undermine the Success of Young Women in the Labor Market."

21. Chao and Bursten, "Girl Talk"; Barbara Borkowska and Boguslaw Pawlowski, "Female Voice Frequency in the Context of Dominance and Attractiveness Perception," *Animal Behaviour* 82, no. 1 (July 2011): 55–59, https://doi.org/10.1016/j.anbehav.2011.03.024.

22. Emma Seppala, "Does Your Voice Reveal More Emotion Than Your Face?" *Greater Good*, June 19, 2017, https://greatergood.berkeley.edu/article/item/does_your_voice_reveal_more_emotion_than_your_face.

23. Michael W. Kraus, "Voice-Only Communication Enhances Empathic Accuracy," *American Psychologist* 72, no. 7 (2017): 644–54, https://www.apa.org/pubs/journals/releases/amp-amp0000147.pdf.

24. University of Michigan, "Persuasive Speech: The Way We, Um, Talk Sways Our Listeners," news release, *EurekAlert!* May 14, 2011, https://www.eurekalert.org/news-releases/530278.

25. Robin T. Lakoff, "'What's Up with Upspeak?" UC Berkeley Social Science Matrix, September 22, 2015, https://matrix.berkeley.edu/research-article/whats-upspeak/.

26. Robin T. Lakoff, "Language in Society," in *Language and Woman's Place* (New York: Harper Torch, 1989), 52–53.

27. "Why Starting Sentences with 'I Feel Like' Is a Conversation Killer," *ParentCo*, May 3, 2016, https://www.parent.com/blogs/conversations/stop-saying-i-feel-like.

28. Maja Jovanovic, "How Apologies Kill Our Confidence," TEDx Trinity Bell Woods Women, February 13, 2019, https://www.youtube.com/watch?v=G8sYv_6uyss.

29. Daina Lawrence, "Women Apologize Too Much in the Workplace and It's Hurting Them," *Globe and Mail*, updated December 23, 2021, https://www.theglobeandmail.com/business/article-women-apologize-too-much-in-the-workplace-and-its-hurting-them/.

30. Sally Helgesen and Marshall Goldsmith, *How Women Rise: Break the 12 Habits Holding You Back* (London: Random House Business, 2019).

Chapter 5: Why Women Don't Speak Up

1. Annie G. Rogers, "Voice, Play, and a Practice of Ordinary Courage in Girls' and Women's Lives," *Harvard Educational Review* 63, no. 3 (Fall 1993): 265–95, https://doi.org/10.17763/haer.63.3.9141184q0j872407.

2. Andrew Littlefield, "Men Are Viewed as Leaders When They Speak Up, but Women Don't Get the Same Benefit," *Convene*, November 21, 2018, https://convene.com/catalyst/office/gender-bias-leadership-voice-feedback/.

3. Jeanette Settembre, "Why Women Are Less Likely to Speak Up in Public than Men," *MarketWatch*, October 3, 2018, https://www.marketwatch.com/story/why-women-are-less-likely-to-speak-up-in-public-than-men-2018-10-02.

4. Francesca Gino, "Why It's So Hard to Speak Up against a Toxic Culture," *Harvard Business Review*, October 30, 2020, https://hbr.org/2018/05/why-its-so-hard-to-speak-up-against-a-toxic-culture.

5. Deborah Tannen, "Do Women Really Talk More than Men?" *Time*, June 28, 2017, https://time.com/4837536/do-women-really-talk-more/.

6. Colleen Flaherty, "The Missing Women," *Inside Higher Ed*, December 19, 2017, https://www.insidehighered.com/news/2017/12/19/study-finds-men-speak-twice-often-do-women-colloquiums.

7. Martin J. Packer and Mark B. Tappan, chapter 7 in *Cultural and Critical Perspectives on Human Development* (Albany: State University of New York Press, 2001), 232–33.

8. Alexandra Knight, in discussion with the author, January 2023.

9. Sheryl Sandberg and Adam Grant, "Speaking While Female," *New York Times*, January 12, 2015, https://www.nytimes.com/2015/01/11/opinion/sunday/speaking-while-female.html.

10. TV Fanatic, "There Is a Land Called Passive Agressiva, and I Am Their Queen . . . ," https://www.tvfanatic.com/quotes/there-is-a-land-called-passive-agressiva-and-i-am-their-queen-ex.html.

11. Lea Winerman, "The Mind's Mirror," *Monitor on Psychology* 36, no. 9 (October 2005): 48, https://www.apa.org/monitor/oct05/mirror.

Chapter 6: Impost-Her Syndrome

1. Savio P. Clemente, "Rising through Resilience: Jessica Doyle on the Five Things You Can Do to Become More Resilient during Turbulent Times," *Authority*, October 8, 2021, https://medium.com/authority-magazine/rising-through-resilience-jessica-doyle-on-the-five-things-you-can-do-to-become-more-resilient-41d02a63adc2.

2. Ruchika Tulshyan and Jodi Ann Burey, "Stop Telling Women They Have Imposter Syndrome," *Harvard Business Review*, February 11, 2021, https://hbsp.harvard.edu/product/H066HL-PDF-ENG.

3. National Archives and Records Administration, "19th Amendment to the U.S. Constitution: Women's Right to Vote (1920)," accessed December 11, 2022, https://www.archives.gov/milestone-documents/19th-amendment.

4. Jessica Hill, "Fact Check: Post Detailing 9 Things Women Couldn't Do before 1971 Is Mostly Right." *USA Today*, October 28, 2020, https://www.usatoday.com/story/news/factcheck/2020/10/28/fact-check-9-things-women-couldnt-do-1971-mostly-right/3677101001/.

5. Brooke Knappenberger and Gabrielle Ulubay, "35 Ways Women Still Aren't Equal to Men," *Marie Claire*, accessed November 8, 2022, https://www.marieclaire.com/politics/news/a15652/gender-inequality-stats/.

6. KPMG, "KPMG Study Finds 75% of Executive Women Experience Imposter Syndrome," news release, October 7, 2020, https://info.kpmg.us/news-perspectives/people-culture/kpmg-study-finds-most-female-executives-experience-imposter-syndrome.html.

7. Leslie Bradshaw, "Why Luck Has Nothing to Do with It," *Forbes*, November 8, 2011, https://www.forbes.com/sites/lesliebradshaw/2011/11/08/why-luck-has-nothing-to-do-with-it/.

8. Nicole Perlroth and Claire Cain Miller, "The $1.6 Billion Woman, Staying on Message," *New York Times*, February 4, 2012, https://www.nytimes.com/2012/02/05/business/sheryl-sandberg-of-facebook-staying-on-message.html.

9. Rebecca J. Rosen, "In the New York Times, Sheryl Sandberg Is Lucky, Men Are Good," *Atlantic*, February 7, 2012, https://www.theatlantic.com/technology/archive/2012/02/in-the-new-york-times-sheryl-sandberg-is-lucky-men-are-good/252686/.

10. Rachel Simmons, "Everyone Fails. Here's How to Pick Yourself Back Up." *New York Times*, accessed December 16, 2022, https://www.nytimes.com/guides/working-womans-handbook/how-to-overcome-failure.

11. Robert Kanaat, "12 Famous People Who Failed before Succeeding," *Wanderlust Worker* (blog), https://www.wanderlustworker.com/12-famous-people-who-failed-before-succeeding/.

12. Kristin Neff, "Self-Compassion Guided Practices and Exercises," Self-Compassion, https://self-compassion.org/category/exercises/.

CHAPTER 7: THE THREE COMMANDMENTS FOR CONQUERING FEAR

1. Carmine Gallo, *Talk Like TED: The 9 Public Speaking Secrets of the World's Top Minds* (New York: St. Martin's Press, 2014), 52–53.

2. Terry Doyle and Todd Zakrajsek, *The New Science of Learning: How to Learn in Harmony with Your Brain* (Sterling, VA: Stylus, 2019), 5–6.

3. Doyle and Zakrajsek, *The New Science of Learning*, 8–10.

4. Megan Schmidt, "This Gene Helps Explain Why Some People Can Get by on Little Sleep," *Discover*, October 17, 2019, https://www.discovermagazine.com/mind/this-gene-helps-explain-why-some-people-can-get-by-on-little-sleep.

5. Matthew Walker, *Why We Sleep* (New York: Scribner, 2017), 6–8.

6. Chiara Cirelli and Giulio Tononi, "Is Sleep Essential?" *PLOS Biology* 6, no. 8 (2008): e216, https://doi.org/10.1371/journal.pbio.0060216.

7. Asher Y. Rosinger, Anne-Marie Chang, Orfeu M. Buxton, Junjuan Lee, Shouling Wu, and Xiang Gao, "Short Sleep Duration Is Associated with Inadequate Hydration: Cross-Cultural Evidence from US and Chinese Adults," *Sleep* 42, no. 2 (February 2019), https://doi.org/10.1093/sleep/zsy210.

8. Bruna Rainho Rocha and Mara Behlau, "The Influence of Sleep Disorders on Voice Quality," *Journal of Voice* 32, no. 6 (2018): 771.e1–771.e13, https://doi.org/10.1016/j.jvoice.2017.08.009.

9. Alison D. Bagnall, Jill Dorrian, and Adam Fletcher, "Some Vocal Consequences of Sleep Deprivation and the Possibility of 'Fatigue Proofing' the Voice with Voicecraft® Voice Training," *Journal of Voice* 25, no. 4 (July 2011): 447–61, https://doi.org/10.1016/j.jvoice.2010.10.020.

10. Walker, *Why We Sleep*, 5, 29, 227.

11. Meredith A. Achey, Mike Z. He, and Lee M. Akst, "Vocal Hygiene Habits and Vocal Handicap among Conservatory Students of Classical Singing," *Journal of Voice* 30, no. 2 (March 2016): 192–97, https://doi.org/10.1016/j.jvoice.2015.02.003.

12. Robert Stickgold and Matthew P. Walker, "Sleep-Dependent Memory Consolidation and Reconsolidation," *Sleep Medicine* 8, no. 4 (June 2007): 331–43, https://doi.org/10.1016%2Fj.sleep.2007.03.011.

13. Walker, *Why We Sleep*, 149–53.

14. Paul King, "How the Brain Decides Which Memories to Hold on To," *Business Insider*, April 14, 2014, https://www.businessinsider.com/how-the-brain-decides-which-memories-to-store-2014-4.

15. John Medina, *Brain Rules* (Seattle, WA: Pear Press, 2008), 33–34.

16. John J. Ratey and Eric Hagerman, *Spark: The Revolutionary New Science of Exercise and the Brain* (New York: Little, Brown, 2013), 45–68.

17. Yuncai Chen, Céline M. Dubé, Courtney J. Rice, and Tallie Z. Baram, "Rapid Loss of Dendritic Spines after Stress Involves Derangement of Spine-dynamics by Corticotropin-Releasing Hormone," *Journal of Neuroscience* 28, no. 11 (March 2008): 2903–11, https://doi.org/10.1523/jneurosci.0225-08.2008.

18. Ratey and Hagerman, *Spark*, 62–64.

19. Wendy Suzuki, "A Neuroscientist Shares the 4 Brain-Changing Benefits of Exercise—and How Much She Does Every Week," CNBC, October 22, 2021, https://www.cnbc.com/2021/10/22/neuroscientist-shares-the-brain-health-benefits-of-exercise-and-how-much-she-does-a-week.html.

20. William J. Lennarz and M. Daniel Lane, *Encyclopedia of Biological Chemistry* (Oxford, UK: Academic, 2013), 331–36.

21. Joshua Gowin, "Why Your Brain Needs Water," *Psychology Today*, October 15, 2010, https://www.psychologytoday.com/us/blog/you-illuminated/201010/why-your-brain-needs-water.

22. Colin Poitras, "Even Mild Dehydration Can Alter Mood," *UConn Today*, February 24, 2012, https://today.uconn.edu/2012/02/even-mild-dehydration-can-alter-mood/.

23. Leslie C. Aiello, "Brains and Guts in Human Evolution: The Expensive Tissue Hypothesis," *Brazilian Journal of Genetics* 20, no. 1 (March 1997), https://doi.org/10.1590/S0100-84551997000100023.

24. Chris Norman, "Feed Your Brain for Academic Success: Boost Learning with Proper Hydration and Nutrition," Healthy Brain for Life, https://www.healthybrainforlife.com/articles/school-health-and-nutrition/feeding-the-brain-for-academic-success-how/.

25. Norman, "Feed Your Brain for Academic Success."

26. Jamie Eske, "Dopamine vs. Serotonin: Similarities, Differences, and Relationship," *Medical News Today*, May 24, 2022, https://www.medicalnewstoday.com/articles/326090#dopamine.

27. Kamiza Garari, "Why Carbohydrates Are Very Important for the Brain," *Deccan Chronicle*, April 23, 2017, https://www.deccanchronicle.com/lifestyle/health-and-wellbeing/230417/why-carbohydrates-are-very-important-for-the-brain.html.

28. Aaron Kandola, "What to Know about Simple and Complex Carbs," *Medical News Today*, May 14, 2009, https://www.medicalnewstoday.com/articles/325171.

CHAPTER 8: COMMANDMENT #2—PINPOINT

1. Rebecca Joy Stanborough, "Understanding and Overcoming Fear of the Unknown," *Healthline*, July 23, 2020, https://www.healthline.com/health/understanding-and-overcoming-fear-of-the-unknown.

2. Carey Marr, Melanie Sauerland, Henry Otgaar, Connie Quaedflieg, and Lorraine Hope, "The Effect of Acute Stress on Memory: How It Helps and How It Hurts," *Inquisitive Mind* 38 (September 2018), https://www.in-mind.org/article/the-effect-of-acute-stress-on-memory-how-it-helps-and-how-it-hurts.

3. Meryl Streep, Instagram, May 20, 2022, https://www.instagram.com/p/CdyhMnopO6y/.

4. Marina Gilman, Alex Rowe, and Peggy Firth, *Body and Voice: Somatic Re-Education* (San Diego, CA: Plural Publishing, 2014), 8–10.

5. Leah Ruppanner, "Women Are Not Better at Multitasking. They Just Do More Work, Studies Show," *Science Alert*, August 15, 2019, https://www.sciencealert.com/women-aren-t-better-multitaskers-than-men-they-re-just-doing-more-work.

6. Kevin P. Madore and Anthony D. Wagner, "Multicosts of Multitasking," *Cerebrum* (April 1, 2019), https://www.ncbi.nlm.nih.gov/pmc/articles/PMC7075496/.

7. Cindy Anderson, "Multisensory Instruction Is Very Important for Our Brains," Hope Springs Behavioral Consultants, July 13, 2019, https://hopesprings.net/multisensory-instruction-brains/; Judy Willis, *Brain-Friendly Strategies for the Inclusion Classroom* (Alexandria, VA: Association for Supervision and Curriculum Development, 2007), 108–11.

Chapter 9: Commandment #3—Power

1. Manfred F. R. Kets de Vries, "How to Find and Practice Courage," *Harvard Business Review*, August 22, 2018, https://hbr.org/2020/05/how-to-find-and-practice-courage.

2. Michael P. Carey and Andrew D. Forsyth, "Self-Efficacy Teaching Tip Sheet," American Psychological Association, 2009, https://www.apa.org/pi/aids/resources/education/self-efficacy.

3. Albert Bandura, "Self-Efficacy: Toward a Unifying Theory of Behavioral Change," *Advances in Behaviour Research and Therapy* 1, no. 4 (1978): 139–61. https://doi.org/10.1016/0146-6402(78)90002-4; Bandura, *Social Foundations of Thought and Action: A Social Cognitive Theory* (Englewood Cliffs, NJ: Prentice-Hall, 1986); Bandura, "Self-Efficacy," in *The Exercise of Control*, 79–113 (New York: Freeman, 1997).

4. Miriam Akhtar, "What Is Self-Efficacy? Bandura's 4 Sources of Efficacy Beliefs," *Positive Psychology*, August 11, 2008, http://positivepsychology.org.uk/self-efficacy-definition-bandura-meaning/.

5. Measure Wellbeing, "General Self Efficacy Scale (GSE)," https://measure.whatworkswellbeing.org/measures-bank/gse/.

6. Nicole Celestine, "4 Ways to Improve and Increase Self-Efficacy," *Positive Psychology*, April 9, 2019, https://positivepsychology.com/3-ways-build-self-efficacy/.

7. Larry G. Maguire, "How to Improve Self-Efficacy: 21 Ways Achieve Your Goals," *Sunday Letters Journal*, October 11, 2019, https://medium.com/sunday-letters-journal/21-ways-to-boost-self-efficacy-achieve-your-goals-9a1ba28dc0cc.

8. Archita Fritz and Olivia Cream, "Episode 36: Choose to Challenge with Your Voice," *Embracing Only* (podcast), July 23, 2021, https://embracingonly.com/episodes/choosetochallengewithvoice-nkrld.

9. Archita Fritz, in discussion with the author, January 2023.

10. Tracy Brower, "Be Brave: How to Build Your Professional Courage," *Forbes*, October 24, 2021, https://www.forbes.com/sites/tracybrower/2021/10/24/be-brave-how-to-build-your-professional-courage/.

Chapter 10: The Deep Dive

1. Melody J. Wilding, "How to Be More Assertive at Work (Not Aggressive)," The Muse, June 19, 2020, https://www.themuse.com/advice/how-to-be-more-assertive-at-work-without-being-a-jerk.

2. Catherine Ashley Sanderson, *Why We Act: Turning Bystanders into Moral Rebels*. Cambridge, MA: Belknap Press, 2022, 68.

3. Tarana Burke, "History and Inception," me too., https://metoomvmt.org/get-to-know-us/history-inception/.

4. Sherri Gordon, "What Is the #MeToo Movement All About?" *Verywell Mind*, April 24, 2022, https://www.verywellmind.com/what-is-the-metoo-movement-4774817.

5. Angela Haupt, "How to Recognize Gaslighting and Respond to It," *Washington Post*, April 18, 2022, https://www.washingtonpost.com/wellness/2022/04/15/gaslighting-definition-relationship-abuse-response/.

6. Heather S. Lonczak, "What Is Gaslighting? 20 Techniques to Stop Emotional Abuse," *Positive Psychology*, August 21, 2020, https://positivepsychology.com/gaslighting-emotional-abuse/.

7. Gabriella M. Filisko, "5 Ways to Communicate Everything Better," *Real Estate Business*, November/December 2021.

8. Brené Brown, "Clear Is Kind. Unclear Is Unkind," October 28, 2021, https://brenebrown.com/articles/2018/10/15/clear-is-kind-unclear-is-unkind/.

9. Joel Garfinkle, "How to Have Difficult Conversations When You Don't Like Conflict," *Harvard Business Review*, May 24, 2017, https://hbr.org/2017/05/how-to-have-difficult-conversations-when-you-dont-like-conflict.

10. Manfred F. R. Kets deVries, "Dealing with Disappointment," *Harvard Business Review*, August 22, 2018, https://hbr.org/2018/08/dealing-with-disappointment.

11. Suzanne Kirch, Ryan Gegg, Michael M. Johns, and Adam D. Rubin, "Globus Pharyngeus: Effectiveness of Treatment with Proton Pump Inhibitors and Gabapentin," *Annals of Otology, Rhinology, and Laryngology* 122, no. 8 (August 2013): 492–95, https://doi.org/10.1177/000348941312200803.

12. UT Southwestern Medical Center, "Silent Reflux," https://utswmed.org/conditions-treatments/silent-reflux/.

13. Sani Penović, Željka Roje, Dubravka Brdar, Sanda Gračan, Ana Bubić, Jadranka Vela, and Ante Punda, "Globus Pharyngeus: A Symptom of Increased Thyroid or Laryngopharyngeal Reflux?" *Acta Clinica Croatica* 57, no. 1 (March 2018): 110–15, https://doi.org/10.20471%2Facc.2018.57.01.13.

14. Liza Torborg, "Mayo Clinic Q and A: Lifestyle Changes May Ease Laryngopharyngeal Reflux," Mayo Clinic News Network, August 1, 2017, https://newsnetwork.mayoclinic.org/discussion/mayo-clinic-q-and-a-lifestyle-changes-may-ease-laryngopharyngeal-reflux.

15. Osborn Head and Neck Institute, "Vocal Hemorrhage Symptoms and Treatment," https://voicedoctorla.com/voice-disorders/vocal-hemorrhage/.

16. Wendy DeLeo LeBorgne and Marci Daniels Rosenberg, "Medicine Myths & Truths," in *The Vocal Athlete: Application and Technique for the Hybrid Singer* (San Diego, CA: Plural Publishing, 2021), 544–45.

17. National Center for Voice and Speech, "Prescriptions," https://ncvs.org/prescriptions/.

18. Jennifer Brett, "Slippery Elm: Herbal Remedies," *How Stuff Works* (blog), February 5, 2007, https://health.howstuffworks.com/wellness/natural-medicine/herbal-remedies/slippery-elm-herbal-remedies.htm.

19. Jennifer Leonard, "Here's How to Get Rid of a Sore Throat Fast," *The List* (blog), June 1, 2020, https://www.thelist.com/213841/heres-how-to-get-rid-of-a-sore-throat-fast/.

Bibliography

Abitbol, Jean, Patrick Abitbol, and Béatrice Abitbol. "Sex Hormones and the Female Voice." *Journal of Voice* 13, no. 3 (September 1999): 424–46. https://doi.org/10.1016/S0892-1997(99)80048-4.

Achey, Meredith A., Mike Z. He, and Lee M. Akst. "Vocal Hygiene Habits and Vocal Handicap among Conservatory Students of Classical Singing." *Journal of Voice* 30, no. 2 (March 2016): 192–97. https://doi.org/10.1016/j.jvoice.2015.02.003.

Aiello, Leslie C. "Brains and Guts in Human Evolution: The Expensive Tissue Hypothesis." *Brazilian Journal of Genetics* 20, no. 1 (March 1997). https://doi.org/10.1590/S0100-84551997000100023.

Akhtar, Miriam. "What Is Self-Efficacy? Bandura's 4 Sources of Efficacy Beliefs." *Positive Psychology*, August 11, 2008. http://positivepsychology.org.uk/self-efficacy-definition-bandura-meaning/.

Akst, Lee. "Phonotrauma." Johns Hopkins Medicine. Accessed August 8, 2021. https://www.hopkinsmedicine.org/health/conditions-and-diseases/phonotrauma.

Alcott, Louisa May. *Little Women*. Baltimore: Penguin, 1953. https://www.scribd.com/read/367159751/Little-Women.

Allen, James. "Gender Bias in Lecture Acoustics." *What I've Learned as a Hospital Medical Director* (blog), November 29, 2019. https://hospitalmedicaldirector.com/gender-bias-in-lecture-acoustics/.

American Speech-Language-Hearing Association. "Vocal Cord Nodules and Polyps." Accessed October 1, 2022. https://www.asha.org/public/speech/disorders/vocal-cord-nodules-and-polyps/.

———. "Voice Disorders." Accessed October 1, 2022. https://www.asha.org/practice-portal/clinical-topics/voice-disorders/.

Amir, Ofer, and Tal Biron-Shental. "The Impact of Hormonal Fluctuations on Female Vocal Folds." *Current Opinion in Otolaryngology and Head and Neck Surgery* 12, no. 3 (June 2004): 180–84. https://doi.org/10.1097/01.moo.0000120304.58882.94.

Anderson, Cindy. "Multisensory Instruction Is Very Important for Our Brains." Hope Springs Behavioral Consultants, July 13, 2019. https://hopesprings.net/multisensory-instruction-brains/.

Anderson, Rindy C., Casey A. Klofstad, William J. Mayew, and Mohan Venkatachalam. "Vocal Fry May Undermine the Success of Young Women in the Labor Market." *PLOS ONE* 9, no. 5 (2014): e97506. https://doi.org/10.1371/journal.pone.0097506.

Arlinghaus, Katherine R., and Craig A. Johnston. "The Importance of Creating Habits and Routine." *American Journal of Lifestyle Medicine* 13, no. 2 (March–April 2019): 142–44. https://doi.org/10.1177%2F1559827618818044.

Aviezer, Hillel, Yaacov Trope, and Alexander Todorov. "Body Cues, Not Facial Expressions, Discriminate between Intense Positive and Negative Emotions." *Science* 388, no. 6111 (November 30, 2012): 1225–29. https://doi.org/10.1126/science.1224313.

Bagnall, Alison D., Jill Dorrian, and Adam Fletcher. "Some Vocal Consequences of Sleep Deprivation and the Possibility of 'Fatigue Proofing' the Voice with Voicecraft® Voice Training." *Journal of Voice* 25, no. 4 (July 2011): 447–61. https://doi.org/10.1016/j.jvoice.2010.10.020.

Bandura, Albert. "Self-Efficacy." In *The Exercise of Control*, 79–113. New York: Freeman, 1997.

———. "Self-Efficacy: Toward a Unifying Theory of Behavioral Change." *Advances in Behaviour Research and Therapy* 1, no. 4 (1978): 139–61. https://doi.org/10.1016/0146-6402(78)90002-4.

———. *Social Foundations of Thought and Action: A Social Cognitive Theory*. Englewood Cliffs, NJ: Prentice-Hall, 1986.

Bender, Rachel Grumman. "Here's What Too-Tight Shapewear Can Actually Do to Your Body." *Self*, March 8, 2017. https://www.self.com/story/what-too-tight-shapewear-can-do-to-your-body.

Bennett, Jessica. "What Do We Hear When Women Speak?" *New York Times*, November 20, 2019. https://www.nytimes.com/2019/11/20/us/politics/women-voices-authority.html.

Bhattacharyya, Neil. "The Prevalence of Voice Problems among Adults in the United States." *Laryngoscope* 124, no. 10 (October 2014): 2359–62. https://doi.org/10.1002/lary.24740.

Biello, David. "Inside the Debate about Power Posing: A Q&A with Amy Cuddy." TED, February 23, 2017. https://ideas.ted.com/inside-the-debate-about-power-posing-a-q-a-with-amy-cuddy/.

Borel, Amy. "What Is Bone Conduction and How Does It Help Us Perceive Sound?" *Forbrain* (blog), June 24, 2021. https://blog.forbrain.com/blog/what-is-bone-conduction-and-how-does-it-help-us-perceive-sound-0.

Borkowska Barbara, and Boguslaw Pawlowski. "Female Voice Frequency in the Context of Dominance and Attractiveness Perception." *Animal Behaviour*

82, no. 1 (July 2011): 55–59. https://doi.org/10.1016/j.anbehav.2011.03.024.

Bradshaw, Leslie. "Why Luck Has Nothing to Do with It." *Forbes*, November 8, 2011. https://www.forbes.com/sites/lesliebradshaw/2011/11/08/why-luck-has-nothing-to-do-with-it/.

Brett, Jennifer. "Slippery Elm: Herbal Remedies." *How Stuff Works* (blog), February 5, 2007. https://health.howstuffworks.com/wellness/natural-medicine/herbal-remedies/slippery-elm-herbal-remedies.htm.

Breus, Michael. "The Relationship between Water and Sleep Health and How to Avoid Dehydration." *The Sleep Doctor* (blog), September 9, 2022. https://www.bipmd.com/news/the-relationship-between-water-and-sleep-health-how-to-avoid-dehydration.

Brower, Tracy. "Be Brave: How to Build Your Professional Courage." *Forbes*, October 24, 2021. https://www.forbes.com/sites/tracybrower/2021/10/24/be-brave-how-to-build-your-professional-courage/.

Brown, Brené. "Clear Is Kind. Unclear Is Unkind." October 15, 2018. https://brenebrown.com/articles/2018/10/15/clear-is-kind-unclear-is-unkind/.

Burcham, Chloe. "13 Celebrities Speak Honestly about Living with PCOS." *Women's Health*, November 12, 2021. https://www.womenshealthmag.com/uk/health/a38171906/celebrities-with-pcos/.

Burgess, Kaya. "Speaking in Public Is Worse Than Death for Most." *Times* (UK), October 30, 2013. https://www.thetimes.co.uk/article/speaking-in-public-is-worse-than-death-for-most-5l2bvqlmbnt.

Burke, Tarana. "History and Inception." me too. Accessed April 17, 2023. https://metoomvmt.org/get-to-know-us/history-inception/.

Burnett, Frances Hodgson. *The Secret Garden*. New York: F. A. Stokes, 1911. https://www.scribd.com/read/479218534/The-Secret-Garden.

Carey, Michael P., and Andrew D. Forsyth. "Self-Efficacy Teaching Tip Sheet." American Psychological Association, 2009. https://www.apa.org/pi/aids/resources/education/self-efficacy.

Celestine, Nicole. "4 Ways to Improve and Increase Self-Efficacy." *Positive Psychology*, April 9, 2019. https://positivepsychology.com/3-ways-build-self-efficacy/.

Chao, Monika, and Julia R. S. Bursten. "Girl Talk: Understanding Negative Reactions to Female Vocal Fry." *Hypatia* 36, no. 1 (2021): 42–59. https://doi.org/10.1017/hyp.2020.55.

Chen, Yuncai, Céline M. Dube, Courtney J. Rice, and Tallie Z. Baram. "Rapid Loss of Dendritic Spines after Stress Involves Derangement of Spine Dynamics by Corticotropin-Releasing Hormone." *Journal of Neuroscience* 28, no. 11 (March 2008): 2903–11. https://doi.org/10.1523/jneurosci.0225-08.2008.

Childs, Leslie. "Voice Care: Sorting Fact from Fiction." *MedBlog*, April 13, 2020. https://utswmed.org/medblog/vocal-cords-care-qa/.

Cirelli, Chiara, and Giulio Tononi. "Is Sleep Essential?" *PLOS Biology* 6, no. 8 (2008): e216. https://doi.org/10.1371/journal.pbio.0060216.

Clemente, Savio P. "Rising through Resilience: Jessica Doyle on the Five Things You Can Do to Become More Resilient during Turbulent Times." *Authority*, October 8, 2021. https://medium.com/authority-magazine/rising-through-resilience-jessica-doyle-on-the-five-things-you-can-do-to-become-more-resilient-41d02a63adc2.

Cleveland Clinic. "Parasympathetic Nervous System (PSNS): What It Is & Function." Accessed January 6, 2023. https://my.clevelandclinic.org/health/body/23266-parasympathetic-nervous-system-psn.

———. "Sympathetic Nervous System (SNS)." Accessed January 6, 2022. https://my.clevelandclinic.org/health/body/23262-sympathetic-nervous-system-sns-fight-or-flight.

Courtney, Rosalba, and Jan Van Dixhoorn. "Questionnaires and Manual Methods for Assessing Breathing Dysfunction." In *Recognizing and Treating Breathing Disorders*, 2nd edition, edited by Leon Chaitow, Dinah Bradley, and Christopher Gilbert, 137–46. London: Churchill Livingstone, 2014. https://doi.org/10.1016/B978-0-7020-4980-4.00012-5.

Coyle Institute. "Your Posture and Your Pelvic Health." Accessed November 30, 2022. https://coyleinstitute.com/your-posture-and-your-pelvic-health/.

Cuddy, Amy. "Your Body Language May Shape Who You Are." TEDGlobal 2012. Accessed March 18, 2023. https://www.ted.com/talks/amy_cuddy_your_body_language_may_shape_who_you_are.

Dhillon, Vaninder Kaur. "Muscle Tension Dysphonia." Johns Hopkins Medicine. Accessed December 16, 2022. https://www.hopkinsmedicine.org/health/conditions-and-diseases/muscle-tension-dysphonia.

Dietrich Maria, Katherine Verdolini Abbott, Jackie Gartner-Schmidt, and Clark A. Rosen. "The Frequency of Perceived Stress, Anxiety, and Depression in Patients with Common Pathologies Affecting Voice." *Journal of Voice* 22, no. 4 (July 2008): 472–88. https://doi.org/10.1016/j.jvoice.2006.08.007.

Doyle, Terry, and Todd Zakrajsek. *The New Science of Learning: How to Learn in Harmony with Your Brain*. Sterling, VA: Stylus, 2019.

Edwards, Kristin Blakemore, "Even Powerful Women Struggle to Speak Up in a Meeting Full of Men: Here's How to Change That." *Inc.*, July 21, 2017. https://www.inc.com/partners-in-leadership/breaking-the-silence-in-the-boardroom-even-when-yo.html.

Ehrmantraut, Jill. "Is Your Breathing Pattern Causing Pelvic Floor Issues?" Apex Physical Therapy and Wellness. Accessed December 20, 2022. https://apexptwellness.com/breath-and-your-pelvic-floor/.

Ellis, Kenneth J. "Human Body Composition: In Vivo Methods." *Physiological Reviews* 80, no. 2 (April 2000): 649–80. https://doi.org/10.1152/physrev.2000.80.2.649.

Eske, Jamie. "Dopamine vs. Serotonin: Similarities, Differences, and Relationship." *Medical News Today*, May 24, 2022. https://www.medicalnewstoday.com/articles/326090#dopamine.

Feldman Barett, Lisa, Batja Mesquita, and Maria Gendron. "Context in Emotion Perception." *Current Directions in Psychological Science* 20, no. 5 (2011). https://doi.org/10.1177/0963721411422522.

Ferris, Emma. "Posture and Breathing: The Physiological Effects of Shallow Breaths." *The Breath Effect* (blog), December 28, 2018. https://www.thebreatheffect.com/posture-breathing-physiological-effects/.

Fessenden, Marissa. "Vocal Fry Creeping into US Speech." *Science*, December 9, 2011. https://www.science.org/content/article/vocal-fry-creeping-us-speech.

Filisko, Gabriella M. "5 Ways to Communicate Everything Better." *Real Estate Business*, November/December 2021.

Flaherty, Colleen. "The Missing Women." *Inside Higher Ed*, December 19, 2017. https://www.insidehighered.com/news/2017/12/19/study-finds-men-speak-twice-often-do-women-colloquiums.

The FootLab. "Knee, Hip & Back Pain: How Foot Posture Affects Our Joints." Accessed December 8, 2022. https://www.thefootlab.com/knee-hip-back-pain-othotics/.

Fritz, Archita, and Olivia Cream. "Episode 36: Choose to Challenge with Your Voice." *Embracing Only* (podcast), July 23, 2021. https://embracingonly.com/episodes/choosetochallengewithvoice-nkrld.

Gallo, Carmine. *Talk Like TED: The 9 Public Speaking Secrets of the World's Top Minds*. New York: St. Martin's Press, 2014.

Garari, Kaniza. "Why Carbohydrates Are Very Important for the Brain." *Deccan Chronicle*, April 23, 2017. https://www.deccanchronicle.com/lifestyle/health-and-wellbeing/230417/why-carbohydrates-are-very-important-for-the-brain.html.

Garfinkle, Joel. "How to Have Difficult Conversations When You Don't Like Conflict." *Harvard Business Review*, May 24, 2017. https://hbr.org/2017/05/how-to-have-difficult-conversations-when-you-dont-like-conflict.

Gilman, Marina, Alex Rowe, and Peggy Firth. *Body and Voice: Somatic Re-Education*. San Diego, CA: Plural Publishing, 2014.

Gino, Francesca. "Why It's So Hard to Speak Up against a Toxic Culture." *Harvard Business Review*, May 21, 2018. https://hbr.org/2018/05/why-its-so-hard-to-speak-up-against-a-toxic-culture.

Goldstein, Joelle. "Amanda Gorman Tells Oprah Winfrey Why Her Speech Impediment Is 'One of My Greatest Strengths.'" *People*, March 25, 2021. https://people.com/human-interest/amanda-gorman-opens-up-speech-impediment-oprah-winfrey-interview/.

Gordon, Sherri. "What Is the #MeToo Movement All About?" *Verywell Mind*, April 24, 2022. https://www.verywellmind.com/what-is-the-metoo-movement-4774817.

Gowin, Joshua. "Why Your Brain Needs Water." *Psychology Today*, October 15, 2010. https://www.psychologytoday.com/us/blog/you-illuminated/201010/why-your-brain-needs-water.

Hassin, Ran R., Hillel Aviezer, and Shlomo Bentin. "Inherently Ambiguous: Facial Expressions of Emotions, in Context." *Emotion Review* 5, no. 1 (January 2013): 60–65. https://doi.org/10.1177/1754073912451331.

Haupt, Angela. "How to Recognize Gaslighting and Respond to It." *Washington Post*, April 18, 2022. https://www.washingtonpost.com/wellness/2022/04/15/gaslighting-definition-relationship-abuse-response/.

Heid, Markham. "What Is Vocal Fry and Creaky Voice?" *Time*, November 2, 2017. https://time.com/5006345/what-is-vocal-fry/.

Helgesen, Sally, and Marshall Goldsmith. *How Women Rise: Break the 12 Habits Holding You Back*. London: Random House Business, 2019.

Hill, Jessica. "Fact Check: Post Detailing 9 Things Women Couldn't Do before 1971 Is Mostly Right." *USA Today*, October 28, 2020. https://www.usatoday.com/story/news/factcheck/2020/10/28/fact-check-9-things-women-couldnt-do-1971-mostly-right/3677101001/.

Hsiao, Tsu-Yu, C. M. Liu, C. J. Hsu, S. Y. Lee, and K. N Lin. "Vocal Fold Abnormalities in Laryngeal Tension-Fatigue Syndrome." *Journal of the Formosan Medical Association* 100, no. 12 (December 2001): 837–40. https://pubmed.ncbi.nlm.nih.gov/11802526/.

Huang, Georgine, "What Has Changed in the Workplace for Women a Year after #MeToo." *Forbes*, October 30, 2018. https://www.forbes.com/sites/georgenehuang/2018/10/30/what-has-changed-in-the-workplace-for-women-a-year-after-metoo/

Hunter, Eric J., Kristine Tanner, and Marshall E. Smith. "Gender Differences Affecting Vocal Health of Women in Vocally Demanding Careers." *Logopedics Phoniatrics Vocology* 36, no. 3 (October 2011): 128–36. https://doi.org/10.3109%2F14015439.2011.587447.

Innis, Jeri. "Anxious or Worried Sick? What's Autonomic Nervous System Dysregulation?" *Innis Integrative BodyMind Therapy*, November 22, 2016. https://www.innisintegrativetherapy.com/blog/2016/11/22/anxious-or-worried-sick-whats-autonomic-nervous-system-dysregulation.

Jurado, Dolores, Manuel Gurpegui, Obdulia Moreno, M. Carmen Fernández, Juan D. Luna, and Ramón Galvez. "Association of Personality and Work Conditions with Depressive Symptoms." *European Psychiatry* 20, no. 3 (May 2005): 213–22. https://doi.org/10.1016/j.eurpsy.2004.12.009.

Kanaat, Robert. "12 Famous People Who Failed before Succeeding." *Wanderlust Worker* (blog). Accessed December 3, 2022. https://www.wanderlustworker.com/12-famous-people-who-failed-before-succeeding/.

Kandola, Aaron. "What to Know about Simple and Complex Carbs." *Medical News Today*, May 14, 2009. https://www.medicalnewstoday.com/articles/325171.

Kets de Vries, Manfred F. R. "Dealing with Disappointment." *Harvard Business Review*, August 22, 2018. https://hbr.org/2018/08/dealing-with-disappointment.

———. "How to Find and Practice Courage." *Harvard Business Review*, May 12, 2020. https://hbr.org/2020/05/how-to-find-and-practice-courage.

Killer, Sophie C., Andrew K. Blannin, and Asker E. Jeukendrup. "No Evidence of Dehydration with Moderate Daily Coffee Intake: A Counterbalanced Cross-Over Study in a Free-Living Population." *PLOS ONE* 9, no. 1 (2014): e84154. https://doi.org/10.1371/journal.pone.0084154.

"Kim Kardashian Passes California 'Baby Bar' Law Exam," BBC News, December 13, 2021. https://www.bbc.com/news/entertainment-arts-59642262.

King, Paul. "How the Brain Decides Which Memories to Hold on To." *Business Insider*, April 14, 2014. https://www.businessinsider.com/how-the-brain-decides-which-memories-to-store-2014-4.

Kirch, Suzanne, Ryan Gegg, Michael M. Johns, and Adam D. Rubin. "Globus Pharyngeus: Effectiveness of Treatment with Proton Pump Inhibitors and Gabapentin." *Annals of Otology, Rhinology, and Laryngology* 122, no. 8 (August 2013): 492–95. https://doi.org/10.1177/000348941312200803.

Knappenberger, Brooke, and Gabrielle Ulubay. "35 Ways Women Still Aren't Equal to Men." *Marie Claire*. Accessed November 8, 2022. https://www.marieclaire.com/politics/news/a15652/gender-inequality-stats/.

KPMG. "KPMG Study Finds 75% of Executive Women Experience Imposter Syndrome." News release, October 7, 2020. https://info.kpmg.us/news-perspectives/people-culture/kpmg-study-finds-most-female-executives-experience-imposter-syndrome.html.

Kraus, Michael W. "Voice-Only Communication Enhances Empathic Accuracy." *American Psychologist* 72, no. 7 (2017): 644–54. https://www.apa.org/pubs/journals/releases/amp-amp0000147.pdf.

Lakoff, Robin T. "Language in Society." In *Language and Woman's Place*, 45–80. New York: Harper Torch, 1989.

———. "'What's Up with Upspeak?" *UC Berkeley Social Science Matrix*, September 22, 2015. https://matrix.berkeley.edu/research-article/whats-upspeak/.

Lawrence, Daina. "Women Apologize Too Much in the Workplace and It's Hurting Them." *Globe and Mail*, updated December 23, 2021. https://www.theglobeandmail.com/business/article-women-apologize-too-much-in-the-workplace-and-its-hurting-them/.

LeBorgne, Wendy DeLeo, and Marci Daniels Rosenberg. *The Vocal Athlete: Application and Technique for the Hybrid Singer*. San Diego, CA: Plural Publishing, 2021.

Lennarz, William J., and M. Daniel Lane. *Encyclopedia of Biological Chemistry*. Oxford, UK: Academic, 2013.

Leonard, Jennifer. "Here's How to Get Rid of a Sore Throat Fast." *The List* (blog), June 1, 2020. https://www.thelist.com/213841/heres-how-to-get-rid-of-a-sore-throat-fast/.

Leonhardt, Megan. "60% of Women Say They've Never Negotiated Their Salary and Many Quit Their Job Instead." CNBC, January 31, 2020. https://www.cnbc.com/2020/01/31/women-more-likely-to-change-jobs-to-get-pay-increase.html.

Littlefield, Andrew. "Men Are Viewed as Leaders When They Speak Up, but Women Don't Get the Same Benefit," *Convene*, November 21, 2018. https://convene.com/catalyst/office/gender-bias-leadership-voice-feedback/.

Lonczak, Heather S. "What Is Gaslighting? 20 Techniques to Stop Emotional Abuse." *Positive Psychology*, August 21, 2020. https://positivepsychology.com/gaslighting-emotional-abuse/.

Lopez, Lukas D., Peter J. Reschke, Jennifer M. Knothe, and Eric A. Walle. "Postural Communication of Emotion: Perception of Distinct Poses of Five Discrete Emotions." *Frontiers in Psychology* 8 (May 2017): 710. https://doi.org/10.3389%2Ffpsyg.2017.00710.

Ludden, Jennifer. "Ask for a Raise? Most Women Hesitate." *All Things Considered*, February 8, 2011. https://www.npr.org/2011/02/14/133599768/ask-for-a-raise-most-women-hesitate.

Madore, Kevin P., and Anthony D. Wagner. "Multicosts of Multitasking." *Cerebrum* (April 1, 2019). https://www.ncbi.nlm.nih.gov/pmc/articles/PMC7075496/.

Maguire, Larry G. "How to Improve Self-Efficacy: 21 Ways Achieve Your Goals." *Sunday Letters Journal*, October 11, 2019. https://medium.com/Sunday-letters-journal/21-ways-to-boost-self-efficacy-achieve-your-goals-9a1ba28dc0cc.

Mahalingam, Shenbagavalli, and Prakash Boominathan. "Effects of Steam Inhalation on Voice Quality-Related Acoustic Measures." *Laryngoscope* 126, no. 10 (October 2016): 2305–2309. https://doi.org/10.1002/lary.25933.

Malde, Melinda, MaryJean Allen, and Kurt Alexander Zeller. *What Every Singer Needs to Know about the Body*. San Diego, CA: Plural Publishing, 2009.

Markham, Heidi. "You Asked: What Is Vocal Fry?" *Time*, November 2, 2017. https://time.com/5006345/what-is-vocal-fry/.

Marr, Carey, Melanie Sauerland, Henry Otgaar, Connie Quaedflieg, and Lorraine Hope. "The Effect of Acute Stress on Memory: How It Helps and How It Hurts." *Inquisitive Mind* 38 (September 2018). https://www.in-mind.org/article/the-effect-of-acute-stress-on-memory-how-it-helps-and-how-it-hurts.

Martins, Regina Helena Garcia, Eny Regina Bóla Neves Pereira, Calo Bosque Hidalgo, and Elaine Lara Mendes Tavares. "Voice Disorders in Teachers.

A Review." *Journal of Voice* 28, no 6 (June 2014). http://doi.org/10.1016/j.jvoice.2014.02.008.

Mayo Clinic. "Aerobic Exercise: How to Warm Up and Cool Down." Accessed December 10, 2022. https://www.mayoclinic.org/healthy-lifestyle/fitness/in-depth/exercise/art-20045517.

McKenzie, Joi-Marie. "Oprah Winfrey Opens Up about Her Battle with Depression: 'I Was behind a Veil.'" ABC News, August 14, 2017. https://abcnews.go.com/Entertainment/oprah-winfrey-opens-battle-depression-veil/story?id=49206090.

McPherson, Susan. "Meet the Winner of the DVF Awards' 2016 People's Voice Award." *Forbes*, May 10, 2016. https://www.forbes.com/sites/susanmcpherson/2016/05/10/meet-the-winner-of-the-dvf-awards-2016-peoples-choice-award/.

Measure Wellbeing. "General Self Efficacy Scale (GSE)." Accessed December 6, 2022. https://measure.whatworkswellbeing.org/measures-bank/gse/.

Medina, John. *Brain Rules.* Seattle, WA: Pear Press, 2008.

Morine, Jared. "How Breathing Can Improve Your Voice." *Speech and Voice Global Enterprises*, January 21, 2020. https://speechandvoice.com/blog/1433/How-Breathing-Can-Improve-Your-Voice.

Myers, Thomas. "Tensegrity." Anatomy Trains. Accessed December 16, 2022. https://www.anatomytrains.com/fascia/tensegrity/.

National Archives and Records Administration. "19th Amendment to the U.S. Constitution: Women's Right to Vote (1920)." Accessed December 11, 2022. https://www.archives.gov/milestone-documents/19th-amendment.

National Center for Voice and Speech. "Prescriptions." Accessed December 19, 2022. https://ncvs.org/prescriptions/.

National Institute on Deafness and Other Communication Disorders. "Taking Care of Your Voice." Accessed December 19, 2022. https://www.nidcd.nih.gov/health/taking-care-your-voice.

Neff, Kristin. "Self-Compassion Guided Practices and Exercises." Self-Compassion. Accessed January 3, 2022. https://self-compassion.org/category/exercises/.

Nestor, James. *Breath: The New Science of a Lost Art.* London: Penguin Life, 2021.

"New Research Reveals Different Perspectives on Workplace Culture." *Los Angeles Business Journal*, June 29, 2021. https://labusinessjournal.com/news/2021/jun/29/new-research-reveals-differences-perspectives-work/.

Norman, Chris. "Feed Your Brain for Academic Success: Boost Learning with Proper Hydration and Nutrition." Healthy Brain for Life. Accessed December 20, 2022. https://www.healthybrainforlife.com/articles/school-health-and-nutrition/feeding-the-brain-for-academic-success-how/.

Ohio State University. "Body Posture Affects Confidence in Your Own Thoughts, Study Finds." *ScienceDaily*, October 5, 2009. https://www.sciencedaily.com/releases/2009/10/091005111627.htm.

Osborn Head and Neck Institute. "Vocal Hemorrhage Symptoms and Treatment." Accessed December 17, 2022. https://voicedoctorla.com/voice-disorders/vocal-hemorrhage/.

Packer, Martin J., and Mark B. Tappan. *Cultural and Critical Perspectives on Human Development*. Albany: State University of New York Press, 2001.

Penović, Sani, Željka Roje, Dubravka Brdar, Sanda Gračan, Ana Bubić, Jadranka Vela, and Ante Punda. "Globus Pharyngeus: A Symptom of Increased Thyroid or Laryngopharyngeal Reflux?" *Acta Clinica Croatica* 57, no. 1 (March 2018): 110–15. https://doi.org/10.20471%2Facc.2018.57.01.13.

Perlroth, Nicole, and Claire Cain Miller. "The $1.6 Billion Woman, Staying on Message." *New York Times*, February 4, 2012. https://www.nytimes.com/2012/02/05/business/sheryl-sandberg-of-facebook-staying-on-message.html.

Poitras, Colin. "Even Mild Dehydration Can Alter Mood." *UConn Today*, February 21, 2012. https://today.uconn.edu/2012/02/even-mild-dehydration-can-alter-mood/.

Ramsower, Stacey. "The Vocal-Vaginal Correlation." *Baby Chick* (blog), August 10, 2021. https://www.baby-chick.com/vocal-vaginal-correlation/.

Ratey, John J., and Eric Hagerman. *Spark: The Revolutionary New Science of Exercise and the Brain*. New York: Little, Brown, 2013.

Rocha, Bruna Rainho, and Mara Behlau. "The Influence of Sleep Disorders on Voice Quality." *Journal of Voice* 32, no. 6 (2018): 771.e1–771.e13. https://doi.org/10.1016/j.jvoice.2017.08.009.

Rogers, Annie G. "Voice, Play, and a Practice of Ordinary Courage in Girls' and Women's Lives." *Harvard Educational Review* 63, no. 33 (Fall 1993): 265–95. https://doi.org/10.17763/haer.63.3.9141184q0j872407.

Rosen, Rebecca J. "In the New York Times, Sheryl Sandberg Is Lucky, Men Are Good." *Atlantic*, February 7, 2012. https://www.theatlantic.com/technology/archive/2012/02/in-the-new-york-times-sheryl-sandberg-is-lucky-men-are-good/252686/.

Rosie, Samantha. "Top 10 Celebrities Known for Their Frequent Use of Vocal Fry." *The Top Tens*. Accessed December 3, 2022. https://www.thetoptens.com/people/people-celebrities-who-use-vocal-fry/.

Rosinger, Asher Y., Anne-Marie Chang, Orfeu M. Buxton, Junjuan Lee, Shouling Wu, and Xiang Gao. "Short Sleep Duration Is Associated with Inadequate Hydration: Cross-Cultural Evidence from US and Chinese Adults." *Sleep* 42, no. 2 (February 2019). https://doi.org/10.1093/sleep/zsy210.

Rowley, Stevie. "The History of Shapewear." *L'Officiel*, August 10, 2022. https://www.lofficielusa.com/fashion/the-history-of-shapewear-spanx-skims-corsets-lingere.

Ruppanner, Leah. "Women Are Not Better at Multitasking. They Just Do More Work, Studies Show." *Science Alert*, August 15, 2019. https://www

.sciencealert.com/women-aren-t-better-multitaskers-than-men-they-re-just-doing-more-work.

Sandberg, Sheryl, and Adam Grant. "Speaking While Female." *New York Times*, January 12, 2015. https://www.nytimes.com/2015/01/11/opinion/sunday/speaking-while-female.html.

Sanderson, Catherine Ashley. *Why We Act: Turning Bystanders into Moral Rebels*. Cambridge, MA: Belknap Press, 2022.

Saunders, Gemma. "How to Take Care of Your Vocal Cords for Singing: Voice Care for Singers." *Open Mic UK*, updated November 13, 2019. https://www.openmicuk.co.uk/advice/how-to-take-care-of-your-voice-and-vocal-cords/.

Schmidt, Megan. "This Gene Helps Explain Why Some People Can Get By on Little Sleep." *Discover*, October 17, 2019. https://www.discovermagazine.com/mind/this-gene-helps-explain-why-some-people-can-get-by-on-little-sleep.

Seppala, Emma. "Does Your Voice Reveal More Emotion Than Your Face?" *Greater Good*, June 19, 2017. https://greatergood.berkeley.edu/article/item/does_your_voice_reveal_more_emotion_than_your_face.

Settembre, Jeanette. "Why Women Are Less Likely to Speak Up in Public than Men." *MarketWatch*, October 2, 2018. https://www.marketwatch.com/story/why-women-are-less-likely-to-speak-up-in-public-than-men-2018-10-02.

Shaw, George Bernard. *Pygmalion*. Mineola, NY: Dover, 1994.

Shuman, Joanna. "Time to Take a Heel Break?" Shuman Podiatry, July 17, 2018. https://shumanpodiatry.com/time-to-take-a-heel-break/.

Simmons, Rachel. "Everyone Fails. Here's How to Pick Yourself Back Up." *New York Times*. Accessed December 16, 2022. https://www.nytimes.com/guides/working-womans-handbook/how-to-overcome-failure.

Sivasankar, Mahalakshmi, and Ciara Leydon. "The Role of Hydration in Vocal Fold Physiology." *Current Opinion in Otolaryngology and Head and Neck Surgery* 18, no. 3 (June 2010): 171–75. https://doi.org/10.1097%2FMOO.0b013e3283393784.

Soukup, Ruth. "Dare to Think Big." In *Do It Scared: Finding the Courage to Face Your Fears, Overcome Adversity, and Create a Life You Love*, 125–26. Grand Rapids, MI: Zondervan, 2019.

Stanborough, Rebecca Joy. "Understanding and Overcoming Fear of the Unknown." *Healthline*, July 23, 2020. https://www.healthline.com/health/understanding-and-overcoming-fear-of-the-unknown.

Stickgold, Robert, and Matthew P. Walker. "Sleep-Dependent Memory Consolidation and Reconsolidation." *Sleep Medicine* 8, no. 4 (June 2007): 331–43. https://doi.org/10.1016%2Fj.sleep.2007.03.011.

Streep, Meryl. Instagram, May 20, 2022. https://www.instagram.com/p/CdyhMnopO6y/.

Suzuki, Wendy. "A Neuroscientist Shares the 4 Brain-Changing Benefits of Exercise—and How Much She Does Every Week." CNBC, October 22, 2021. https://www.cnbc.com/2021/10/22/neuroscientist-shares-the-brain-health-benefits-of-exercise-and-how-much-she-does-a-week.html.

Tallon, Tina. "A Century of 'Shrill': How Bias in Technology Has Hurt Women's Voices." *New Yorker*, September 3, 2019. https://www.newyorker.com/culture/cultural-comment/a-century-of-shrill-how-bias-in-technology-has-hurt-womens-voices.

Tannen, Deborah. "The Truth about How Much Women Talk—and Whether Men Listen." *Time*, June 28, 2017. https://time.com/4837536/do-women-really-talk-more/.

Tavel, Morton E. "Hyperventilation Syndrome: A Diagnosis Usually Unrecognized." *Journal of Internal Medicine and Primary Healthcare* 1 (2017). http://doi.org/10.24966/IMPH-2493/100006.

Torborg, Liza. "Mayo Clinic Q and A: Lifestyle Changes May Ease Laryngopharyngeal Reflux." Mayo Clinic News Network, August 1, 2017. https://newsnetwork.mayoclinic.org/discussion/mayo-clinic-q-and-a-lifestyle-changes-may-ease-laryngopharyngeal-reflux.

Tulshyan, Ruchika, and Jodi Ann Burey, "Stop Telling Women They Have Imposter Syndrome." *Harvard Business Review*, February 11, 2021. https://hbsp.harvard.edu/product/H066HL-PDF-ENG.

TV Fanatic. "There Is a Land Called Passive Agressiva, and I Am Their Queen. . . ." Accessed December 27, 2022. https://www.tvfanatic.com/quotes/there-is-a-land-called-passive-agressiva-and-i-am-their-queen-ex.html.

University of Michigan. "Persuasive Speech: The Way We, Um, Talk Sways Our Listeners." News release. *EurekAlert!* May 14, 2011. https://www.eurekalert.org/news-releases/530278.

UT Southwestern Medical Center. "Silent Reflux." Accessed December 13, 2022. https://utswmed.org/conditions-treatments/silent-reflux/.

Voice Science Works. "SOVT Exercises." Accessed September 18, 2022. https://www.voicescienceworks.org/sovt-exercises.html.

Walker, Matthew. *Why We Sleep*. New York: Scribner, 2017.

"Why Starting Sentences with 'I Feel Like' Is a Conversation Killer." *ParentCo*, May 3, 2016. https://www.parent.com/blogs/conversations/stop-saying-i-feel-like.

Wilding, Melody J. "How to Be More Assertive at Work (Not Aggressive)." The Muse, June 19, 2020. https://www.themuse.com/advice/how-to-be-more-assertive-at-work-without-being-a-jerk.

Wilhelm, Kay, Gordon Parker, Liesbeth Geerligs, and Lucinda Wedgwood. "Women and Depression: A 30 Year Learning Curve. *Australian and New Zealand Journal of Psychiatry* 42, no. 1 (January 2008): 3–12. https://doi.org/10.1080/00048670701732665.

Willis, Judy. *Brain-Friendly Strategies for the Inclusion Classroom*. Alexandria, VA: Association for Supervision and Curriculum Development. 2007.

Winerman, Lea. "The Mind's Mirror." *Monitor on Psychology* 36, no. 9 (October 2005): 48. https://www.apa.org/monitor/oct05/mirror.

Winter, Lottie. "Every Single One of Kim Kardashian West's Businesses—from Dash to Skims—Ranked." *Glamour UK*, September 13, 2022. https://www.glamourmagazine.co.uk/gallery/kim-kardashian-businesses.

Index

About the Author

Jessica Doyle-Mekkes is a wife, girl mom, beach bum, aspiring foodie, and Broadway superfan. She's also the head of musical theatre at East Carolina University, where she has taught since 2017. A vocal coach, researcher, and accomplished performer, she has spent the last fifteen years studying the power of the human voice.

Jessica is an internationally published writer and sought-after clinician for both singers and public speakers. Her work uniquely combines brain science, voice science, and girl power. She is passionate about teaching women how to harness the power of their voices: in their heads and out of their mouths. Her goal is to help all women create a clear, confident voice that is authentically theirs and then to use that voice fearlessly.

Jessica lives in Greenville, North Carolina, with her husband, Don; their daughters, Tallulah and Jolie; and a codependent chihuahua named Sebastian.

Printed in the USA
CPSIA information can be obtained
at www.ICGtesting.com
CBHW030951260724
12226CB00002B/8

9 781538 179161